AF342648

YEARS OF PROMISE

YEARS OF PROMISE
THE UNIVERSITY OF UTAH'S
A. RAY OLPIN ERA, 1946–1964

ANNE PALMER PETERSON

FOREWORD BY DAVID P. GARDNER

THE UNIVERSITY OF UTAH PRESS
Salt Lake City

 The Defiance House Man colophon is a registered trademark of the University of Utah Press. It is based upon a four-foot-tall, ancient Puebloan pictograph (late PIII) near Glen Canyon, Utah.

13 12 11 10 09   1 2 3 4 5

LIBRARY OF CONGRESS CATALOGING-IN-PUBLICATION DATA
Peterson, Anne Palmer, 1962-
Years of promise : the University of Utah's A. Ray Olpin era, 1946-1964 / Anne Palmer Peterson.
    p. cm.
Includes bibliographical references and index.
 ISBN 978-0-87480-969-5 (cloth : alk. paper) 1. University of Utah—History—20th century. 2. Olpin, Albert Ray, b. 1898. 3. University of Utah—Presidents—Biography. I. Title.
LD5533.P48 2009
378.792'258—dc22
            2009027547

Printed and bound by Sheridan Books, Inc., Ann Arbor, Michigan.

All photographs are courtesy of Special Collections, J. Willard Marriott Library, University of Utah.

Contents

Foreword

Anne Palmer Peterson's biography of A. Ray Olpin is not only an informed, insightful, and engaging account of one man's journey as president of the University of Utah, it is also an exposition of the pivotal years between 1946 and 1964. And Ms. Peterson tells this story well, drawing on primary sources and archival materials not previously published, Olpin's personal journals and papers, and the recollections of those who knew Olpin or worked with him during his years at the university. The reader gains a heretofore-unappreciated view of the man and his contributions as Peterson clearly and forthrightly details the challenges Olpin faced within the broader cultural, social, economic, political, and religious environment of mid-twentieth-century Utah.

Before venturing into the story of Olpin's presidency, it may be useful to know something more about the position of university president and the expectations various parties have of those who hold it. Clark Kerr, former president of the University of California, described these best in his famous 1963 Godkin lectures at Harvard University:

> The university president in the United States is expected to be a friend of the students, a colleague of the faculty, a good fellow with the alumni, a sound administrator with the trustees, a good speaker with the public, an astute bargainer with the foundations and the federal agencies, a politician with the state legislature, a friend of industry, labor, and agriculture, a persuasive diplomat with donors, a champion of education generally, a supporter of the professions (particularly law and medicine), a spokesman to the press, a scholar in his own right, a public servant at the state and national levels, a devotee of opera and football equally, a decent human being, a good husband and father, an active member of a church. Above all he must enjoy traveling in airplanes, eating his meals in public, and attending public ceremonies. No one can be all of these things. Some succeed at being none.[1]

---

1. Clark Kerr, *The Uses of the University,* 4th ed. (Cambridge, MA: Harvard University Press), 1995), 22.

Olpin succeeded at being most of these things, serving for more than eighteen years when the average period of service for university presidents in America lasted only five. Length of service is one thing; accomplishment is quite another, of course. Olpin satisfied both criteria, and the Peterson biography explains how he did it.

Olpin's task awaited his arrival and required action, not just reflection. World War II had just ended, and America's universities were in for a big change. Olpin knew this, had been thinking about it, and undertook without hesitancy or much conversation with others a course of primarily self-defined and self-driven initiatives. These were designed to transform the University of Utah from a small, respected, mostly liberal-arts state institution into a major American public university with the threefold mission of teaching, research, and public service. He sought to accommodate within its student body a growing share of Utah's talented young people, thus enhancing educational opportunities for aspiring and prepared students and assuring a growing pool of well-educated and trained people for Utah as the state anticipated a future less rooted in agriculture and more attuned to the coming technological and scientific revolutions.

The nation was also seeking to recover from the adverse effects of World War II. Government and university partnerships forged during the war needed to be fostered and broadened to extend the benefits of basic and applied research to peacetime endeavors. The enactment by Congress of the GI Bill of Rights with its provision for student financial aid for veterans also promised more immediate changes for the nation's colleges and universities as millions of veterans sought to commence or complete their studies at the war's end.

Thus, when Olpin, at age forty-seven, and his wife, Elva, and their family arrived in Salt Lake City in 1945 from his post as director of the Ohio State University Research Foundation, the strategic challenge was self-evident: to recruit and support a faculty suited to his sense of the university's future and to develop a nationally recognized program of graduate studies and research, the latter mostly dependent upon the former.

He succeeded in ways that even today must be regarded with astonishment.

Although these objectives may have been clear to Olpin, they were far from obvious to many within the state of Utah. This concept of a new "U" had not been seriously contemplated within the power centers of Utah, given the region's comparative isolation, small population, and scarce resources.

For Olpin these apparent barriers were merely affirming reasons to put such changes into place, lest Utah fail to advance toward the future but rather hold onto the past at this pivotal moment in the nation's history. Peterson's biography chronicles, describes, interprets, and illuminates the way Olpin swung the university's gates toward a more encompassing, rather than constricted, future. This important recognition of the potential for the university was driven in no small measure by Olpin's vision, tenacity, courage, and powers of persuasion. His presidency not only transformed the "U" (laying the foundations and footings for its ensuing structure) but also helped set the state on a course more attuned to what was coming next, rather than what was remembered but nevertheless left behind.

From Olpin's point of view, opportunity mostly masqueraded as a problem. A lesser man would have failed to make the distinction. Or, if he had discerned it, he would have shied away. Not this president.

Peterson's accounts of Olpin's encounters with Governor J. Bracken Lee, business and professional interests in the state, and others, including some people on his governing board, whose views were not always congruent with his own, makes for good reading. They also provide real insight into Olpin's style and personality. Most importantly, they make readers aware of the depth and breadth of his commitment to the university whose interests and needs he so ably served for nearly two decades. Here are just a few examples:

- Peterson's account of Olpin in 1946 personally persuading General Dwight David Eisenhower to take down the fence separating the campus from underutilized facilities at Fort Douglas and use them instead for university needs is a real classic. The university desperately needed these facilities to cope with the influx of thousands of students. More importantly, the story demonstrates the way Olpin worked and why he was so successful in most of his endeavors. (This first step onto Fort Douglas land was a coup.)

- Her accounts of Olpin's battles with Governor J. Bracken Lee over funding are stunning. Olpin's restraint was only matched by Lee's "over the top" attacks, not only on the university but on Olpin personally. Nevertheless, Olpin didn't back down but pressed even harder, not just with Lee but also with key legislators, alumni, and other friends who tried to help, and did. In the end, Olpin prevailed, and he and Lee actually became friends.

- Peterson's account of the trials and tribulations of building a four-year medical school during the mid-1940s is fascinating. She describes the ways that Olpin and the medical-school staff were resisted in this effort by many doctors in private practice, hindered by internal disagreements, burdened with grossly inadequate facilities and funding, and opposed by many legislators and a public skeptical about the costs to taxpayers. Olpin persevered nevertheless and succeeded against overwhelming odds in bringing this dream to fruition.

- Peterson's description of Olpin's efforts to attract nationally known scientists and scholars to the faculty in line with his vision is a story of unexpected successes and a wily president who used every tool at hand, including the influence of the spouses of those recruited, to achieve his objective. The roster of those hired is truly impressive and a tribute to Olpin's vision and determination. For those whom he recruited, it was also an act of faith to leave secure positions in other universities to join the University of Utah at this critical, changing, and uncertain time.

- Peterson vividly describes Olpin's large and overloaded desk, stacked high with reports, correspondence, memoranda, and minutia, reflecting the understaffed reality of the president's position, a result of unsympathetic funding by the state. Olpin determined in spite of it all to get the job done.

- Peterson's various accounts of Olpin's interaction with leading institutions in the state and with their leaders helps the reader appreciate the range and diversity of interests with which he was obliged to work. She reports these encounters frequently and faithfully, thus helping readers appreciate even more the level of dedication Olpin brought to the "U," the way he subordinated his needs to those of the university, and his willingness to press on even when situations became inconvenient and, in some vivid instances, job threatening.

- Olpin's conduct was courageous during the McCarthy era in the early 1950s, when many of our nation's colleges and universities considered or adopted faculty loyalty oaths. The most famous example occurred at the University of California, where the implementation of such an oath in 1949 wreaked havoc on that institution. Olpin simply said, "There will be no loyalty oaths in this university as long as I am president, and that's that," according to Professor Sterling McMurrin. McMurrin goes on to describe Olpin as a "tower of strength in absorbing blows that were directed against the faculty for its honesty in teaching and its forthrightness in speaking out on crucial issues."[2]

---

2. Sterling M. McMurrin, "From Innocence to Sophistication," in *Remembering the University of Utah,* ed. Elizabeth Haglund (Salt Lake City: University of Utah Press, 1981), 197.

Without Olpin's contributions, without his successes, without his unstinting and unwavering dedication to and belief in the University of Utah, the "U" would be a very different place today. By way of example, there would be no major health-sciences center on campus; there would be no professional schools or colleges in medicine, pharmacy, or nursing; and most of the university's other professional schools, graduate programs, and research centers and institutes would be nonexistent.

The student body would be only a fraction of its current size, resulting in the loss of talent to the state because the ablest of the young would have chosen to study elsewhere. The physical plant would have been hopelessly inadequate for the needs of an early twenty-first century major university, being devoid of research laboratories, sophisticated equipment, major computer facilities, clinics for the care of medically needy people, and a library possessing the knowledge base required for serious scholarship, among other things.

Now for some more personal reflections. I met President Olpin when I joined the University of Utah family as its tenth president in 1973. Olpin had concluded his presidency nine years earlier. He was kind enough to visit me within a few weeks of my arrival, sharing generously and helpfully the things he knew about the "U" and the state and many of its key personalities. Because I was new to Utah, he helped me understand the university/state relationship, the university/LDS Church interaction, and the connection between the university and businesses, alumni, and donors.

Olpin shared a story that told me all I needed to know about the university's relationship with the LDS Church. Several years earlier he had attended a play at Kingsbury Hall. The drama included a lively drunk scene, and Olpin observed that an apostle of the LDS Church, who was also there, seemed to appreciate this part of the play less than the rest of it. Sure enough Olpin received a phone call the following day from the apostle who, Olpin said, "expressed his dismay and disappointment that the 'U' had allowed a drunk scene in what was an otherwise fine play."

Olpin added that within the next hour, he had received a second call, this time from then LDS Church President David O. McKay. President McKay had called to congratulate Olpin on the university's staging such a fine production and asked about the young actor who had played the part of the drunk, observing that "it was not easy to play such a part convincingly." McKay then went on to say, according to Olpin, how much he had enjoyed the play and complimented the university's theater program in general.

"Dave," Olpin said, "there it is—few things in life are monolithic, including the LDS Church. Persons of the same faith do not always believe the same thing about everything, even theologically, not to mention everything else." It was good advice.

During most of my presidency at the "U," Lillian Ence was my secretary/executive assistant and made my life bearable. She had worked in the Park Building during most of the Olpin years and told me this story: Olpin parked his car in front of the Park Building as usual. But on this particular day, the gardener turned on the water for the lawn in that area just as Olpin was getting out of his car. He and his car were greeted with a drenching as a result.

Olpin went to the gardener to tell him to turn off the water. The gardener said that he couldn't because this was the time the water was supposed to be turned on for this area. Olpin, exasperated and dripping, said something like, "Do you know who I am?" The gardener demurred. "Well then," Olpin continued, "who is your boss?" The gardener named his immediate supervisor. "And who is his boss?" Olpin persisted. The grounds' worker named his supervisor's supervisor. This went on until he finally reached the person in charge of the university's grounds and buildings. "And who is the director's boss?" Olpin asked, expecting himself to be the answer. The gardener replied, "The director's the big boss, and he don't report to anyone." With that answer in hand, a dejected Olpin walked into the Park Building with the water still running, shared the story with Lillian and others, shed his very wet coat, entered his office with a sigh, and began his day.

President Olpin then shared with me the disappointment he felt during his emeritus years at not being invited to enjoy the social, cultural, intellectual, and athletic events that he had so cherished during his presidency. Driving had become prohibitive.

After that the Olpins were invited to all university functions Libby and I hosted where they would feel welcome and at ease. They were assured of tickets to cultural and athletic events and informed about special lectures and similar intellectual opportunities open to the public. I arranged for a university car to pick them up and return them home from such events. It pleased me very much to see both President and Mrs. Olpin at the basketball and football games a couple of rows up from our section, at Pioneer Theatre and Kingsbury Hall performances, at dinners honoring special guests, at official functions, and at commencement, where Olpin was always introduced to much applause.

Others, before Olpin and since, have helped make the "U" what it is today. Many talented people on the faculty and the staff served in both his administration and mine. But it was A. Ray Olpin, seventh president of the University of Utah, who envisioned the school's potential more than a half century ago.

A reading of Peterson's biography will help us remember not only what he accomplished but also what one man with a sense of history and a vision for the future can do. Leadership does make a difference.

—David Pierpont Gardner
President Emeritus
University of Utah
University of California

Acknowledgments

The aim of this book is to fill an important gap in the recorded history of the University of Utah. Why that gap exists is an interesting story.

Three other authors began the history of the University of Utah's Olpin era before I started to work on this manuscript. Previous versions were intended to be more biographical than this account. A faculty committee preparing to celebrate the bicentennial of the Declaration of Independence commissioned one pair of writers in 1974. They were to collaborate with President A. Ray Olpin on his memoirs.

I have undertaken a less panoramic view of Olpin while still emphasizing the aspects of his work that were most important to him. These were chosen based on close textual analysis of archival records and historical recovery work. Olpin expressed his candid views in daily notes that he recorded beginning in the second year of his presidency. They read more like a personal diary than an office journal. No wonder he was hesitant to turn these journals over to the university. Past researchers also provided me with notes from their interviews with Olpin after his retirement. Combining these sources gave me access to Olpin's keenest memories. Many entries focused upon his most trying encounters. Thankfully, these dusty records were preserved for thirty years by Elinore Partridge and then turned over to me. These personal papers furnished insights beyond the administrative records in the university archive.

Boyer Jarvis has been the driving force behind efforts to document the A. Ray Olpin years, when the University of Utah experienced its greatest development and growth. He encouraged many donors to financially support the publication of this book. I thank him, along with Presidential Special Assistant Laura Snow and Vice President for Institutional Advancement Fred Esplin, for involving me.

University archivist Kirk Baddley has been an indomitable resource in helping to gather the material for this text. Kirk's appreciation for the role of the university's history in its continuing welfare is impassible. I am grateful for his frankness and insight.

A student, Donald G. Williams, also aided me in my research at the Marriott Library. He was astute in his work and will be an asset to library science.

The once and future historian, and emeritus director of the American West Center, Floyd O'Neil, helped me to see this project in its political contexts. Everett Cooley's oral-history collection enabled me to hear the voices of its subjects. The John F. Kennedy Library Foundation provided me with the Arthur M. Schlesinger Jr. fellowship, which expanded the scope of my research. That library's archives in Boston permitted me to trace A. Ray Olpin's links to the Peace Corps—making this more of an American story.

This undertaking would not have been possible without the patient support of my family. My parents, Joseph and Dorothy Ann Palmer, gave me cause to reflect upon the University of Utah's history in the first place. Their courtship took place there during the A. Ray Olpin years. Thank you also to my husband, Peter, for encouraging my relationship with the seventh president of the University of Utah for the past four years.

CHAPTER 1

PUTTING THE PIECES INTO PLACE

Albert Ray Olpin, his wife, Elva, and their two youngest children, Virginia, thirteen, and Howard, nine, were to arrive in Salt Lake City either on the twentieth, twenty-first, or twenty-third of December in 1945. Crossing the country mandated an undetermined number of stops for the Olpins. The actual date of their departure from their home at 2045 Wickford Road in Columbus, Ohio, was unknown to colleagues awaiting Olpin's arrival. What was known is that the Olpins were expected to be guests of honor at a New Year's Day reception hosted by University of Utah President LeRoy E. Cowles and his wife in honor of Cowles's successor. The January 1 gala had been planned at the Student Union—a building that would be replaced in a new location eleven years after Olpin's presidency began. The new Student Union would eventually be named after the university's postwar president, A. Ray Olpin, but the honorary name was not bestowed until 1972, eight years after his retirement.

The Olpins were returning to Utah with their four children after a twenty-two-year absence. They had never anticipated living so long away from their home state. Now, six months after the end of World War II, Olpin was anxious to inspire in students the desire to handle responsibly the world's most destructive weapon. The Manhattan Project had combined the forces of science, government, academia, the military, and industry into an organization that had taken nuclear physics from the laboratory onto the battlefield. This clarified the importance of basic scientific research to national defense. Work at Ohio State University's Research Foundation

After earning his Bachelor of Arts degree in 1923 from Brigham Young University, Olpin taught physics and math there for a year.

Olpin and his wife, the former Elva Chipman, welcome baby Helen Rae, the first of their four children.

had exposed Olpin to the classified scientific and political details behind America's building of the atom bomb. That job had given him the opportunity to see the possible relationship between government needs and educational resources. He had begun to realize that the postwar role of the university could melt away the ivory towers. Universities had gained the potential to become a new kind of resource for government, business, and industry. Olpin was a physicist, and World War II had ended up being a physicist's war. Upon leaving Ohio State, Olpin had been cited by the War Department for his individual contribution to the Manhattan Project.[1] He was accustomed to accolades and accustomed to success.

A. Ray Olpin had received offers for teaching fellowships from both Columbia University and the University of California during his first year as an instructor at his alma mater, Brigham Young University (BYU). There, in Provo, Utah, he had access to guidance from the highest ranks of the private, church-owned school. He had met his future wife, Elva Chipman, there, and the university instilled in them its motto: "The glory of God is intelligence." BYU's president, Franklin S. Harris, told Olpin that a young man from the West would do well to complete his education in the East.[2]

Accepting that advice, the freshman instructor, his wife, and their one-year-old daughter, Helen, moved to New York. Olpin enrolled as a graduate student and signed on as a teaching assistant at Columbia University. With his dissertation, "Method of Enhancing the Photoelectric Emission from Alkali Metals," he earned his Ph.D. in physics seven years later. Freshly minted, Dr. Olpin was so interested in new developments within the communications industry and so excited by his possibilities at Bell Telephone Laboratories that he decided to remain in the East indefinitely. It was a high-profile place to land. Olpin had a home for his family built in Bayside, New York.

In 1933 the textile industry captured Olpin's attention. A laboratory directorship in Charlotte, North Carolina, held sufficient appeal to draw the Olpins into the South. Olpin had the opportunity to build a laboratory and introduce new research methods to the staid cotton industry. He remained there for five years as director of research at the Kendall Company. He then went on to the Ohio State University Research Foundation, where he ended up as director.

Because of their lineage, leaving Utah had been a difficult choice for the Olpins. A. Ray had been born in the same Pleasant Grove home as his father, a house built by his father's father. His wife and her family were well known in the region. Her father managed the Chipman Department Store in American Fork, and her grandfather had been the first Utah secretary of state. They were married during Olpin's junior year at BYU. Both were faithful followers of the Church of Jesus Christ of Latter-day Saints, which had its worldwide headquarters about fifty miles north of Provo in Salt Lake City. A. Ray even shared the legacy of a June 1 birthdate with Brigham Young, the prophet who had led church pioneers on their exodus to Utah. Some of his parents' friends and relatives had even wanted him to share the name. However, his mother did not want a name that could be reduced to a ridiculing nickname—"Brig" or "Ham," perhaps. The brief name Ray seemed to defy attempts to shorten it, so it was coupled with his father's name, Albert. Musing about his given name in Sapporo, Japan, while on his LDS mission, Olpin wrote that he found the initial and his middle name rather poetic when combined in his signature.[3]

When Elva and Ray, their family, and furnishings returned to Utah for their Salt Lake City debut, there was no university president's home to house them. In fact, they were competing with a flood of fighting men returning home from the war, all of them searching for lodging amidst a housing crisis. The Olpins arranged to rent Eben R. T. Blomquist's home at 70 University Street. The house wasn't ready that December, so Howard Beale, professor emeritus of business, arranged to take the Olpins in. Their furniture was put into storage in the basement of the campus library.

A picture of Olpin stepping out of the family's black Oldsmobile sedan in his gray hat, wearing a white shirt, striped tie, and well-fitted overcoat, was front-page news in the *Salt Lake Telegram's* December 22, 1945, edition. Readers who had known A. Ray in Pleasant Grove saw that Olpin now wore a thin, salt-and-pepper moustache and wire-rimmed eyeglasses. At forty-seven, his hair was more gray than brown beneath the hat's narrow brim. Naturally news of his arrival was reported in the *Provo Daily Herald,* where Olpin had worked as an occasional reporter, and in *The Pleasant Grove Review.* It had been his practice to send the editors press releases and local-boy-makes-good clippings about his professional accomplishments while living back East. The *Kaysville Weekly Reflex, Morgan County News, Bountiful Clipper, Moab Times Independent, Murray Eagle, Bingham Bulletin, Logan Cache American,* and *Coalville Bee* carried news of his arrival, too.

Albert Ray Olpin, seventh president, led the University of Utah for eighteen and a half years.

In 1945 the president of the University of Utah, the president of the LDS Church, and the governor were the state's leading dignitaries—even if the University of Utah still lacked the stature of a major public university. That would come. It was Olpin who truly laid the foundations of the modern University of Utah. Congress and President Franklin D. Roosevelt's cabinet were catalysts. They had been contemplating postwar recovery plans since 1943, but the GI Bill's passage the following year took college leaders by surprise. While wartime planners gave indications that teaching methods and curricula were bound for change, education leaders had precious little involvement with the way this educational expansion would take place in a peacetime society. Some felt that veterans attending college under the Servicemen's Readjustment Act would reduce academic standards. Higher education would become less a privilege and more an entitlement.

With its generous tuition and subsistence allowance, the GI Bill caused academic upheaval in the United States. Many outspoken college and university presidents contributed to the turmoil. This watershed coincided with A. Ray Olpin's only university presidency.

While America was fraught with postwar giddiness and anxiety, Olpin, with his scientific training and a vision of the role universities could play in a new industrial

ABOVE: The Union Building, opened in 1957 during his presidency, would not be named for Albert Ray Olpin until eight years after his retirement.

LEFT: President Olpin tipped the pins at the grand opening of the new Union Building in 1957.

society, demonstrated neither. The most pressing problem facing the University of Utah at the end of the war was inadequate facilities to accommodate the former fighting men. Many of them also had families to house. During his first year as president, Olpin had to cope with an 84 percent increase in university enrollment over the previous year. In the fall of 1945, fewer than 5,000 students had clustered between classes on the plaza of the Park Building at the apex of the horseshoe now known as President's Circle. Nearly one-third of them were freshman girls in green beanies. Nine buildings surrounded the horseshoe; twenty-three buildings made up the entire campus. The university had 225 full-time faculty members. The eighteen men in the university's administration included the manager of the bookstore and the superintendent of buildings and grounds. There had never been a vice president. The university offered little more than a good liberal-arts education and teacher training: it provided only minimum service to the state's citizens. It had the most inadequate student housing of any state university in the West.[4] Because A. Ray Olpin was the kind of person who thrived on challenge, rather than complained of a crisis, he perceived the situation as a superb opportunity to make his mark. Changes were in order, scaled to the president's ambitions.

By 1946–47, the total University of Utah enrollment had increased to 9,859; the allocation from the state legislature, however, was based upon an enrollment of 3,200 to 3,500 students. By 1949 the student body had risen to 12,050, plus another

Fort Douglas Station Hospital became Central Hall dorm for men in 1946 and remains in use for University administration.

5,515 students registered for extension courses. In 1951 veterans still made up one-third of the university student body. Upon Olpin's retirement from the University of Utah in 1964, long-range planning was under way to accommodate more than 20,000 students.[5]

The end of World War II fueled the demand for education, but the growth in enrollment at the University of Utah did not subside once the veterans had graduated. Olpin's job not only required unusual administrative, organizational, and personal skills, but seemed to call for a magician's act: the ability to materialize objects—in this case, buildings and teachers—from thin air with no sure knowledge of where to obtain them or who would provide the necessary funds.

By statute the University of Utah had to admit any student who was a high-school graduate. By intention neither the regents nor the governor wanted to turn away any qualified student. After the war, applications poured in, overwhelming the teaching and administrative staffs, who wondered where the rooms for all the classes could be found. Olpin tightened scholastic standards, prohibiting acceptance of out-of-state students possessing anything below a B average. Still, the university was bulging at the seams. Meanwhile, the U.S. Army's Ninth Service Command was vacating facilities at nearby Fort Douglas. In an action that presaged his ability to capitalize quickly on unforeseen opportunities, new president A. Ray Olpin

During World War II, Fort Douglas' Cummings Field was the site of close order drilling for soldiers in the Army Specialized Training Unit. Photo: 1943.

found a way to make a pitch for Fort Douglas buildings and property.

General Dwight D. Eisenhower, then the U.S. Army's chief of staff, came to Salt Lake City to consult with local military and civic leaders on February 18, 1946. He intended to inspect various military posts, including particularly the Tooele Ordnance Depot and Hill Air Force Base, the morning newspaper reported. The general had announced that he would be too busy for any unscheduled meetings. Olpin was fond of recounting the story: "He [Eisenhower] said that he didn't want anybody to seek interviews with him, because he had all he could do to spend one day here going all around, out to Tooele, and around to Hill Field, and all those places, to inspect the various military posts. But I wanted to talk to him about those buildings, in Vancouver, Washington, Vermont, Wyoming, out in Tooele and so on, about using them for housing. I thought that if we could get some of these from Fort Douglas it would be a whole lot easier."[6]

Olpin knew that the university's original founders in 1850 had marked out a campus of more than six hundred acres but that some of the designated bench land had been lost to military operations through three separate acts of Congress. And, since 1919, University officials had been spreading the word around Washington that acquiring land from the Fort Douglas Reservation would be necessary to expand the campus.[7] Olpin was determined to leverage the mutual interest that he and Eisenhower shared for the welfare of young men and women who had interrupted their education to defend their country. He was also determined to recapture Fort Douglas for the university.

The army and the university were like siblings contesting an inheritance. Officials with the city of Salt Lake and leaders of the Veteran's Administration had their sights set on the Fort Douglas land, too. As expressed on several occasions by Major General William E. Shedd, commander of the Ninth Service Command, there was strong sentiment in the army, supported by a statutory directive, against civilian use of military facilities. Although Eisenhower had been talking about decentralizing control of unused housing facilities at various command posts, army officials wanted to retain title to Fort Douglas. Their preference was to permit the National Guard and other government agencies to use the now-excess land,[8] which was highly desired by government workers being

Veterans attending the U lived in barracks formerly housing the Women's Army Corps.

squeezed out of downtown by a shortage of office space. However, Olpin and the university's Board of Regents saw the living quarters and training grounds at the neighboring base as the only way to ease the overcrowded conditions on campus that ironically veterans were causing. Seizing the opportunity to present the university's case in person, Olpin requested a meeting with Eisenhower.

The president was in a faculty meeting when his secretary entered and handed him a note. General Eisenhower would see him at five o'clock in his room at the Hotel Utah. Olpin abruptly turned over the gavel and drove down South Temple Street. Upon entering the hotel, Olpin saw that Salt Lake City Mayor Earl J. Glade had also been offered an audience with Eisenhower. Olpin recalled the showdown: "I've never seen so much brass in my life. There were colonels and generals of every station at every turn. I knocked on the door, and a colonel or somebody answered. I told him who I was and that General Eisenhower wanted to see me."[9]

Eisenhower greeted him cordially, acknowledging, "I understand that you have more students than you know what to do with." Olpin said, "That's very true."[10] Eisenhower then explained that he wanted General Shedd, who would be vacating Fort Douglas for a new position at the California Presidio military post, to move over and accommodate the university's pressing needs.

Eisenhower then described a meeting the previous day with his brother, Milton Eisenhower, president of Kansas State University, who was struggling with a similar inundation. After hearing from Olpin that little more than a few yards and a fence

By 1958, as many as 2,000 students at a time were taking classes in the Annex.

separated the University of Utah from the army base at Fort Douglas, the general declared, "Cut a hole in the fence and let the boys through!"[11]

Major General Shedd still objected, citing a federal law prohibiting civilian use of army posts. General Eisenhower replied, "That law will be changed when I get to Washington. I've fought with those boys; I crossed the Channel with two million of them. They're good boys, and I have great affection and respect for them. Let them have everything you can—extra facilities, supplies and furniture—nothing's too good for them."[12]

In early March 1946, General Shedd did turn over to the university thirty acres east of the campus. The buildings located there were used to house single veterans. In April forty-eight more family units were allocated.

That fall the four-story Building No. 105, which later became known simply as "the Annex" (formerly Ninth Service Command headquarters), and twenty-one other buildings were granted to the university. Several federal agencies also wanted Building No. 105. Even officers in the War Assets Administration sought the building for a regional office. These were the officials who were meant to oversee disbursement of what had been built up.[13] Utah Governor Herbert B. Maw sent a telegram to Eisenhower, reminding him that at the Governors' Conference in Oklahoma City, Eisenhower and President Truman had indicated that accommodating veterans should take priority in such cases. "Therefore," the governor wrote, "I respectfully urge that you issue instructions that Building 105 be made available to the University of Utah for the education of 2,000 G.I.'s."[14]

The wooden buildings acquired from the fort had holes in the floors, and they wore no "skirts" for insulation around their cement-block foundation posts.[15] A rowdy student could easily punch holes in the walls of the narrow, crowded hallways lined with soft paper-composition wallboard. Students often did. The long, low-ceilinged design severely obstructed sightlines to the chalkboard. Some stairways had to be made one directional. This helped to keep them from becoming jammed during class breaks. The Annex was a dirty, cramped firetrap, but it was deemed the only army building suitable for college classrooms, and to the university, it represented a real coup.[16]

The Annex's location—so far south and east from the buildings clustered around the horseshoe—created a new planning dilemma. It was more than a mile away from the main campus. The traffic system at the university was unable to accommodate the increased load, so the temporary solution for lessening congestion was constructing a road between the Annex and the main campus.[17]

The arrangement allowing the university temporary use of the buildings on the lower fort property continued until 1947. Olpin did not like being dependent upon the federal government for assistance in solving the university's problems.[18] He had already cut his teeth by negotiating for nearly half a million dollars worth of army surplus equipment to use in teaching labs while heading the Research Foundation at Ohio State.[19]

Amending the law so that the university could acquire, rather than borrow, the land and buildings required first building political consensus. The Utah delegation in Congress, led by Senator Elbert D. Thomas, who chaired the Military Affairs Committee, gave invaluable support and assistance in procuring this tract for the university. Buttressed by the university's Board of Regents, Olpin made lobbying for the land transfer one of his chief tasks. His tone in the letters and telegrams to elected officials ranged from pleading—simply to rent or lease the run-down barracks—to cajoling and eventually demanding that the land be turned over "in light of our emergency needs."[20] Had he been more understated in tailing the Federal Public Housing Authority, relieving the congestion by acquiring the fort probably would not have occurred. Rising to the times, Olpin was a peerless campaigner.

Between the spring of 1946 and September of 1948, Olpin and the state's congressional delegation put pressure on the War Assets Administration, the Federal Public Housing Authority, the director of War Mobilization and Reconversion, the Federal Works Agency Bureau of Community Facilities, the U.S. Office of Education, President Truman, and the secretary of war.[21] Olpin was fully focused on ensuring that the university would fall heir to the post, either by grant or purchase. In these diligent efforts, the university administration was aided by state and civic leaders, orchestrated by the Salt Lake Chamber of Commerce. Lawmaking efforts to amend the Surplus Property Act by Senators Elbert Thomas, Abe Murdock, and Arthur V. Watkins finally opened the way for the university to acquire the land and buildings declared surplus by the army.[22] Then, whether the university even possessed the legal status to accept the land, was contested.

Included in the contract were rights to the Fort Douglas golf course, which, according to Olpin, had "definite educational recreational value, as well as providing a buffer to protect the forest preserves and the community from grass fires."[23] With aid once again from the state's elected officials, a deal was struck with the club's equity members to permit faculty, the university student golf team, and a limited number of students with advanced golfing skills to play the eighteen-hole course. The 1947 agreement noted that if expansion required the university to build upon the course, the club's members would have to pay to realign the fairways.[24] When club members began playing instead at the Hidden Valley Golf Club in Draper, the old Fort Douglas course was left in the university's hands. Olpin remembered that club members were tough negotiators and quite unhappy about losing the course, with its scenic view of a growing downtown Salt Lake skyline.[25]

The old Fort Douglas hospital was remodeled into a men's dormitory, and some of the barracks were turned into men's housing as well. The university saved money in furnishing the dormitory rooms when the navy vacated the Field House, which had been used since 1943 as a "big bedroom" for army and navy personnel in the specialized-training reserve program. The navy sold its used beds and mattresses to the university for 20 to 50 percent of their cost.[26]

To house married students, Stadium Village was assembled from thirty surplus barracks that the Federal Public Housing Authority brought to Salt Lake City from the Japanese internment camps at Topaz, Utah, and Van Port, Oregon. Hill Field and the Ogden Arsenal in Ogden, the Tooele Ordnance Depot, and the Basic Magnesium Plant in Henderson, Nevada, provided other sources of surplus buildings. The university and the Public Buildings Administration paid to remodel and move them. Construction on the project came to a halt in December 1946 when the Federal Public Housing Administration determined that cities ought to be responsible for campus emergency veteran housing projects. Olpin went to Washington to make another of his successful appeals.

President Olpin, Assistant Secretary of State for Far Eastern Affairs Dean
Rusk, Head of the Department of Military Science and Tactics Hubert Cole,
and Dean Arthur Beeley, discussing U.S. foreign policy on October 24, 1950.
In 1961, Olpin told Rusk that he thought President Kennedy had plagiarized
his Peace Corps plan.

The complex, north of the football stadium, grew to include 301 units occupied by more than a thousand men, women, and children.[27] Five percent were faculty. The university's Veterans Housing Committee kept a long waiting list of families hoping to secure one of the tiny residences. Rent was twenty-five dollars for one room with kitchen and bath, forty-five dollars for a two-bedroom unit, and fifty dollars for a three-bedroom unit.[28] Amenities provided by the university included fenced play areas with shaded sandboxes.[29]

With students' families living in such close proximity, a crippling outbreak of polio occurred at the "U." A survivor, LaVelle Eastman, the wife of a veteran fighter pilot, recalled life in Stadium Village during the summer of 1951: "We slept on a hide-a-bed in the living room, rented a cot for our son, and had a baby in the crib in the bedroom. We didn't have a tub, so I bathed the baby in the kitchen sink. While we were living there, our son Alan contracted polio. There was a big epidemic in the village. He was five. I couldn't get a babysitter to watch my baby, not a neighbor or a friend. I couldn't leave to go anywhere, they were so afraid of us."[30]

Also, in November 1948, the university received title to nearly 300 acres of Fort Douglas land in the military reservation west of Wasatch Boulevard. The War

Olpin remained involved with the university after retiring. Pictured in 1965, left to right, are Academic Affairs Vice President Jack Adamson, Olpin, University President James C. Fletcher, Board of Regents Chair Royden Derrick, and Business Vice President Paul Hodson.

Assets Administration presented the deed to the property to the university—at no cost to the state. Generally called the lower parade ground, it included sixty-one buildings on the fort grounds and forty-five buildings off site to be moved to university property. This addition brought the university's holdings to 447 acres. It was the largest single land acquisition for the university since 1850, and it helped bring the land base more nearly back to the original design of the founders and forward to fulfill the needs of 1950.

The additional land provided immediate emergency relief for swollen postwar enrollments because with it eventually came a hundred wooden buildings. The buildings were bare, however. Those who took classes following the close of the war often found themselves sitting on high stools or the floor, or even standing at the back of their classrooms. And while students were using their knees as writing desks, the U.S. Army had, in storage, several thousand tablet armchairs, some of which had never been used. Although it seems simple and obvious to provide the students with chairs, cutting through the red tape tying up the army surplus required determination, aggressiveness, farsightedness, and the ability to take advantage of unexpected opportunities. These were among the attributes of the university's new president, and he saw to it that he received credit for his efforts.

Another telephone call to General Eisenhower finally released eighteen hundred chairs from the fort for students to use. "Every time a door opened, I was there to get something for the U. of U.," Olpin said.[31]

Land, buildings, and chairs alone do not make a university. A more pressing matter was finding teachers to meet the demands for advanced educational opportunities, particularly in the professions. When he accepted the position as president, Olpin had two major goals: to recruit a first-rate faculty and to develop nationally recognized graduate and research programs. If he managed to achieve these primary goals, Olpin felt, he would have established the basis for a fine university.

Chapter 2

Bringing Professors Along

In an ambitious faculty recruitment program that continued into the early 1950s, President Olpin sought some of the best people in the country in various fields. The home the Olpins were renting at 1259 East South Temple Street was in nearly constant use for faculty recruitment and, at commencement time, for student receptions as well. At first Olpin went after faculty with whom he had been associated in the sciences and research. Rather than taking the orthodox approach of choosing whoever was available, Olpin sought to build a faculty with enough stature and credibility to attract research contracts. To accomplish this goal, he sought teachers of national or international distinction. He strongly believed that not only should the university aspire to attract the best but that funding top-notch faculty was the most economical policy for the state. It was preferable, he showed, to bring a great scholar to many students in Utah than to send a few Utah students east or west in search of graduate or professional training.

President Cowles and College of Medicine Dean Cyril Callister had made inroads into this new way of thinking during the war. Their "heroic" decision to start a four-year medical school at Utah had broken through psychological and economic barriers that had previously insulated the state from outside influence and helped maintain its historic provincialism.[1] Olpin told prospective hires that "we are a research-minded institution. Our College of Medicine alone attracts over $350,000 per year in the way of private foundation and government grants for the support of research. It is outstanding in the nation and ranks among the top half-dozen university medical schools."[2]

Sterling M. McMurrin served as U.S. commissioner of education under President John F. Kennedy from 1961 to 1962. While at the University of Utah, he was academic vice president, dean of the graduate school, and a professor of philosophy and history.

Roger Bailey, who helped plan the new campus as well as develop the Department of Architecture, came from the University of Michigan.

Among the many faculty members hired in Olpin's early years were O. Meredith Wilson from the University of Chicago, E. Adamson Hoebel from New York University, L. David Hiner from Ohio State University, and Armand Eardley from the University of Michigan. Also from Michigan came Roger Bailey, who helped plan the new campus, as well as develop the Department of Architecture, and Avard Fairbanks, who became resident sculptor and dean of the School of Fine Arts. Jesse D. Jennings, a National Park Service archaeologist working in Omaha, was an early recruit, as was a Utah alumnus who had already established a reputation as an outstanding scholar, Sterling McMurrin, who was teaching philosophy at the University of Southern California. These were just a few of the academics hired by Olpin who were instrumental in building the programs and reputation of the University of Utah. They were singled out for recognition in 1949 by G. Homer Durham, director of the Institute of Government and, later, the university's first vice president of academic affairs.[3]

Olpin felt confident that he could lead and orchestrate similar improvement in other fields. In fact, he was determined to do so. He was often asked to speak on such subjects as "The Impact of War Research on the Average Citizen." He discussed the effects of such developments as radar, sonar, penicillin, and DDT. The president was convinced that surrounding himself with others who held similarly broad views would benefit the state. He began his recruitment efforts his first week in office by trying to entice Princeton University's Henry Eyring to head the University of Utah's research effort.[4] Olpin told the Board of Regents that Eyring was "internationally famous, one of the best chemists in the country…a mathematician, chemist, physicist, biologist, metallurgist, and author" as well.[5] With the aim of building a major research program at the university, he proposed that Eyring be invited to be dean of the graduate school. Heretofore, there had been no graduate school, only a graduate division.

To head the newly created College of Mines and Mineral Industries, Olpin set his sights on Carl J. Christensen, head of the Chemical Research Department and a seventeen-year employee of Bell Telephone Laboratories. To appoint Christensen dean, Olpin obtained permission from the Administrative Council in May and the Board of Regents in June 1946. "If we could get two good men like these who are really known, then we would be 'on our way' here in Utah," Olpin told the Board of Regents.[6]

He knew both men personally and professionally. Christensen he had known all of his life, and Eyring's uncle, Carl Eyring, had been Olpin's professor at Brigham Young University. Olpin felt that they might be lured to Utah by their desire to live closer to their church's headquarters, as well as participate in the expansion of the University of Utah. Olpin tested the Board of Regents' attitudes toward having professorships partly subsidized by industries. He emphasized that an institution is no bigger than the "men" in its departments. The Board of Regents' meeting minutes record his statement: "Men are what make the school."[7]

Following the appointments of Eyring and Christensen, some of those on the faculty and the board complained of a Mormon invasion, harkening back to the Kingsbury days. Olpin said, "Anytime I can't appoint an outstanding scientist because he's a Mormon, I'll quit."[8] He wrote to Eyring, "I try not to consider religious affiliation in any of my appointments."[9]

Henry Eyring's appointment in chemistry reflected Olpin's focused effort. Eyring was known internationally for his formulation of the theory of rate processes in chemical reactions, and professors at Princeton marveled that such a man could be attracted to a place like Utah. The dean of the Princeton graduate school stated, "In the field of theoretical chemistry, Henry Eyring is probably the greatest mind developed in this age, or perhaps any age."[10]

Princeton University relinquished Professor Henry Eyring, who joined Utah's chemistry department and headed the graduate school.

In early 1946, President Olpin visited New Jersey, where he offered Eyring the position of head of Utah's graduate school. Eyring was in his scientific heyday. He had published two influential textbooks, *The Theory of Rate Processes* and *Quantum Chemistry*. He had been elected to the academically elite National Academy of Sciences. Eyring respectfully declined Olpin's offer and suggested that he hire Carl Christensen instead.[11] The next day his wife, Mildred Bennion Eyring, told Henry that she and their three sons were moving back to her home in Utah with or without him. Eyring quickly decided to accept the eight-thousand-dollar-per-year job, and he and his family arrived in Salt Lake City later that summer.[12]

Many wrongly assumed that whatever Utah had gained would be a loss to science. Eyring himself expressed sadness at leaving behind many promising graduate students at Princeton. However, he continued to publish, lecture, attend conferences, and develop new ideas from his Utah base. Furthermore, he attracted brilliant students and faculty from all over the country. His appointment as professor of chemistry and dean of the new graduate school was instrumental in giving the University of Utah increased visibility and a national reputation.

In June 1948, the first Ph.D. degrees at the university were conferred, one in chemistry and one in pharmacology. With Eyring's reputation for scholarship

James Sugihara earned the University of Utah's first doctorate in 1947 and went on to teach chemistry.

and scientific research, the graduate school assumed national importance as early as 1950. More University of Utah students were earning doctorates in mining and metallurgy than in any other department.[13] An Institute of Rate Processes under the codirection of Eyring and Carl J. Christensen also attracted national attention. All this acted as precedent, encouragement, and stimulus. The end result of this accumulation of talent was that the number of faculty more than doubled to more than five hundred teachers by 1950.

Olpin was in a unique position to take advantage of the money becoming available in quantity to universities with research facilities and distinguished faculty. Ohio State had been one of the first universities to receive cooperative research grants. There Olpin had acquired the insight to appreciate the relationship possible between industry and a university. He was prepared to further leverage the federal financing that had streamed into Utah during World War II. Defense spending had dramatically improved Utah's economy and taught local politicians vital lessons about the value of positive relationships with bureaucrats in Washington. Utah's location, far from the ports of the West Coast but accessible by rail, highway, and air, had given it a strategic advantage during the war. Olpin planned to capitalize on those wartime investments as the nation began its rapid economic rise.[14]

He insisted that research provide a seedbed for industry. And for the university to stage a full-scale venture into the academic field of graduate study required that it become a research institution, undertaking sponsored, or cooperative, projects.[15] The state's greatest need, he said, was putting trained men to work in laboratories solving problems that research had brought to the people's attention.[16]

Attracting top-name professors meshed with his plan to match Utah's increased level of intellectual activity to the research and grant monies becoming available through the federal government and industry. He felt certain these research grants would become an important source of income for universities in the 1950s and '60s, and they did. In 1946 grant monies received by the university for basic research amounted to $183,525. By 1963 that figure had increased to $10,122,317.

What were Utah's attractions for the scholars and researchers who responded to Olpin's petitions? His own reputation was one factor. Many who came knew him personally or professionally and trusted his vision and drive. Others respected his attitude toward research and his interest in developing a graduate program. Many who came were returning home again. After establishing careers and reputations elsewhere, they and their families welcomed the opportunity to return to the mountains and valleys where they had deep roots.

"There are many people from Utah and the entire West whose backgrounds and living are as sound and sturdy as the pioneers; and there are many people in the world who look to the west for guidance," wrote Avard Fairbanks from Ann Arbor when considering Olpin's invitation to return.[17] Reflecting upon his decision a few years later, he said, "I suppose that all Utahns wish to return to their home state particularly when they feel an urgent need for their work."[18]

Utah's reputation for relatively clean, dry air was an incentive for those whose wives or families had chronic asthma or other respiratory problems. For almost a year, Olpin corresponded with Clarence R. Wylie, a brilliant mathematician, before he was able to persuade Wylie to come and head the math department. Instrumental in their negotiations was the fact that Wylie's wife had a serious sinus condition. In his letters to Wylie, Olpin discussed salary, fringe benefits, and several cases where respiratory problems had been dramatically relieved when the sufferers had moved to Utah.

Some were excited by the challenge and opportunity to become involved in the expansion and intellectual growth that they saw occurring. Utah's resources, culture, and history were of interest not only to metallurgists and engineers but also to anthropologists, archaeologists, sociologists, and historians. Many Olpin-era faculty members came planning a short stay but grew to love the country and the people and became permanent residents.

Citing some of these advantages, Olpin sent personal letters to recruit people whom he knew or had heard about and wanted to bring to Utah. To those unfamiliar with the state, he adopted the tone of a public-relations promoter, noting that everyone who passed through Salt Lake City or lived there seemed to fall in love with the place. The climate, he said, was ideal; the streets, wide and clean; the schools, first in the nation; and the recreational opportunities in the surrounding canyons, unsurpassed in both summer and winter.

Olpin also went to great lengths to obtain money for the higher salaries that top out-of-state professors often commanded. He also created positions that he felt would give the faculty power and influence. Enticing Harold W. Bentley from Columbia University involved complex negotiations on both position and salary. As Bentley responded when he was first approached, "Columbia is a place one doesn't

Harold Bentley, head of the Extension Division, led the university's team of educational consultants to Haile Selassie I University in Ethiopia.

toss over lightly."[19] Juggling various funding sources and possible positions, Olpin finally was able to hire Bentley simultaneously as dean of the summer school, director of the Humanities Foundation and the University Press, and professor of English.[20]

Bentley, whom Olpin had met through the LDS Church while living in New York, also responded to some of the inducements already described. His letter of acceptance acknowledged them: "I suppose that most of us sons of the Utah region fondle the idea of returning some time and are pleased when we are invited to do so. We seem to have a weakness for wanting to participate in the shaping of an institution which our convictions prompt us to think have promising opportunities for importance and greatness."[21]

Bentley was born in Mexico to Utah-connected parents who were living just across the river from El Paso, Texas, in Colonia Juarez in the state of Chihuahua. He attended Utah Agricultural College for two years, then transferred to Brigham Young University. After earning his doctorate from Columbia, Bentley became the assistant director of Columbia University Press, moved to Mexico City to become director of the Benjamin Franklin Library, and then returned to Columbia, where he directed both the press and the bookstore. Olpin wrote Bentley that the university needed him to "pioneer" its rapidly expanding humanities program.[22]

Olpin corresponded extensively with prospective faculty members and took great personal interest in their families. He helped them find housing, answered questions about getting their children into schools, gave them detailed information about fringe benefits, and offered to help store furniture and books until housing could be arranged. O. Meredith Wilson wrote that he was concerned about his appointment being announced in the local papers before he had had a chance to inform his mother in Utah that he was coming. Olpin offered to call her as soon as the university's Board of Regents approved his appointment.

In 1946 Olpin reorganized the old School of Mines and Engineering to become two colleges: the College of Engineering and the College of Mines and Mineral Industries. As a research scientist, Olpin knew that the field was shifting from conventional, hard-rock mining to the uses of nonmetallic minerals such as uranium, vanadium, beryllium, and silicon. He maintained that no state had better nonmetallic resources for the new aerospace age than Utah. He was determined to make the university's mining school the most prominent in the nation—a place to which the state's industries would come for guidance.

As an administrator and businessman, Olpin had often remarked on the inefficiency of mining raw materials, taking them out of the state for processing, and then bringing them back into Utah as finished products. In fact, he had identified this as one of the key problems confronting the state and the university when he was being interviewed for his position as president. He had told the faculty that Utah could not afford to continue shipping out raw materials for processing and then buying them back, fabricated, for a much higher price than the mining companies had received for the raw materials. He felt that the University of Utah should assist in developing industrial resources and provide information and know-how to create new industries. He lamented to the Board of Regents that "some of the biggest names in the mining industry, scattered throughout the country, were graduates of Utah and lost to the State."[23]

While directing research at Ohio State, Olpin had kept close counsel with Clyde E. Williams, director and later president of Battelle Memorial Institute, headquartered in Columbus. Olpin developed a great deal of respect for Williams, who was responsible for correlating various aspects of government metallurgical research. He discovered that Williams had graduated from the University of Utah and asked him why he'd never mentioned his Utah education. Williams replied he had not thought it important because the University of Utah had little national recognition in his own field of metallurgy; his Utah diploma seemed to contribute little to his reputation.

Olpin insisted that research provided by the University of Utah could dramatically aid the economy of the entire state. Dean Carl Christensen, with seventeen years' experience in mineral and metallurgical research engineering at Bell Telephone Laboratories, shared Olpin's vision to lead the college in effecting change. The university could not only meet postwar industrial demands but also enlist the support of private industry to expand its capacity. A university development fund had been set up to receive a $200,000 gift from Kennecott Copper Corporation for basic research in mining and ore development. Kennecott executives specified

Gown meets town at a 1947 meeting of the American Society of Mining Engineers. Left to right, Salt Lake Mayor Earl Glade, Olpin, E. W. O'Brien, Governor H. B. Maw, metallurgist Clyde E. Williams of Ohio, J. Calvin Brown, and C. E. Davis.

that the funds should focus on the extraction and processing of the mineral resources abundant in the intermountain region.

At first the increased emphasis on research and graduate programs dismayed the leading mining industrialists of the state. They could see no need for the high-powered graduate program or training experts in the practical and theoretical uses of the "new" materials. "We don't want Ph.D.'s leaning on shovels," Board of Regents Chairman William J. O'Connor told Olpin.[24] O'Connor was the general manager of American Smelting and Refining Company.

Yet Christensen and Olpin pushed forward with plans to create a first-class curriculum of study in physical metallurgy while waiting for a fabricating industry to develop around the metals mined and smelted in Utah. In just a few years, the new college was bringing into the state money in the form of research grants, industrial processing and products, and new firms, whose directors were attracted by the program at the University of Utah. Olpin invited his old Ohio friend Clyde Williams back to Utah to receive an honorary doctorate. In accepting the degree, Williams said, "Today, I can't give a better reference than my degree from the University of Utah," which showed just how much his attitude about his alma mater had changed.

The College of Mines and Mineral Industries was becoming one of the country's best. The college's growing visibility exemplified a dramatic shift in the prestige of the University of Utah. Olpin "wanted to develop the human as well as the mineral resources of the state."[25]

Olpin leveraged this desire into a new pay system to aid him in reorganization and future recruitment. He knew that salaries would have to be increased and that he would meet with opposition not only from the state legislature but also from some of the entrenched faculty members. Leveraging the federal government's compensation under the GI Bill of Rights on the basis of per-student credit-hour cost, Olpin was able to increase faculty salaries by one-sixth in one year. By changing faculty contracts from three quarters over twelve months to four quarters per year, he enabled faculty members to receive added compensation from sponsored contracts for the quarter when they were not teaching.[26] He required faculty members to teach three terms and use the fourth for research or self-improvement. This helped both to attract new teachers and professionalize teaching by increasing research productivity.[27] Longtime faculty had become accustomed to a system of stratified salaries based upon rank and determined by years of service. Some resented the prospect of "outsiders" coming in at higher salaries. Those devoted primarily to teaching worried that the increased emphasis on research would threaten their interests or even their positions on the faculty.

In one case of deep unrest, members of the engineering faculty objected to Olpin's selection of outsider Samuel S. Kistler, "a scientist, and not an engineer," to head the College of Engineering.[28] They argued vociferously that Olpin's designee would be unable to "meet the requirements of professional men downtown." And they resented the fact that Olpin had not canvassed the current faculty to consider promoting one of its members to be dean. Olpin prevailed; Kistler was hired away from the private chemistry lab he was running in Massachusetts, and he served through the president's retirement. Three indignant members of the engineering faculty quit in protest. Mervin B. Hogan, whom Kistler appointed head of the Department of Mechanical Engineering, was later demoted for insubordination. Yet Olpin insisted that the faculty resolve its own conflicts; he saw these as petty annoyances. At the crux of the matter was the university's escalating link to industry.

Kistler wrote about the need for a new building to unify the far-flung departments of the College of Engineering, scattered across campus in temporary buildings. He and Olpin saw eye-to-eye about the university's new role in Utah's changing economy. Kistler wrote,

> The conviction that agriculture has contributed only a minor share to present prosperity, that mining must inevitably decline in relative importance and that manufacturing and trade will eventually be the mainstay of Utah's economy, is gaining support in important circles. There is no doubt but that there will be a close connection between industrial development in the state and the demand for technically trained personnel. It is our belief that by proper organization of industrial backing for new engineering facilities…in the event that the legislature cannot be persuaded of our need for funds, we believe that the industry served by our students can well provide them.
>
> A new sense of the responsibility of industry toward education has been developing in the past twenty years. Far-sighted companies realize that the corporation, as a hypothetical citizen, must take the place of the wealthy private citizen of generations past in providing funds for education.[29]

Kistler went on to recommend that each corporation acknowledge the university's contribution to its productivity by donating $3,000 per technically trained University of Utah alumnus it employed. Had the dean's plan for private financing been successfully implemented, the 112 engineers of the 1953 graduating class would have brought $336,000 into the college. In three years, enough could have been raised to finance the construction of a new building.[30]

To such financial and internal challenges were added others, sometimes stemming from political or religious pressures. Olpin was determined to remain blind to a person's religion in making hiring decisions. Duane G. Hunt, bishop of the Utah Catholic diocese, visited him to complain that there were too few Catholics on the faculty. Olpin told him that he had no idea what the percentage of Catholics was because he'd never inquired about the religion of his faculty members. His hiring policies, he emphasized, did not include examining religious affiliation. Olpin offered to give the bishop a list of the professional qualifications included in the job descriptions he was then drafting. "Find people who will meet our requirements," Olpin told the bishop. "If they're really good, we may hire them, but we'll never ask about their religious affiliation."[31] According to Parry Sorensen, public-relations director under Olpin and a former FBI investigator, Olpin did follow up on Hunt's complaint by recruiting chemistry professor William Burke—a devout Roman Catholic who was teaching at Ohio State.[32]

It was a little disingenuous for Olpin to profess ignorance of faculty members' religious persuasion. Even applicants brought up the subject. Another chemist, W. Conrad Fernelius, broached the issue amidst job negotiations: "There are some other matters which I would not want to be an embarrassment to you. As far as I know I am the only Utah Fernelius who is not a member of the LDS Church. It is not that I am antagonistic but simply that I never found it possible to accept all of their doctrines. I am a Congregationalist and am greatly interested in church ideals."[33]

Fernelius told Olpin he was also a Mason, an organization that in Utah formally prohibited Mormon membership. This was Olpin's response to Fernelius's forthright revelations:

> Although many people here are concerned with the religious beliefs of staff members, no appointments are made on the basis of a man's religion. My policy is to appoint the best man for the job and let the others do the worrying about where he worships. It is only natural that perhaps a large percentage of the people on the faculty should be Mormons, but there are many departments which are predominantly non-Mormon. You should be in an unusual position to attract the support of all, for I believe you would understand both groups. Incidentally, I think the most militant group of faculty members are the non-Mormon group, and it is only natural that they should be on the defensive most of the time, for they represent the minority group in the community.[34]

Adding to all these pressures were the inevitable controversies resulting from honest scholarship and free inquiry. "Whenever you bring in a real scholar," Olpin observed at the university's centenary celebration, "there's bound to be someone unhappy with his views."[35] Yet real scholars needed the assurance that their institution would, in Olpin's words, "provide a climate [allowing them] to utilize their talents as free-thinking individuals."[36] George Thomas, president of the University of Utah from 1921 to 1941, had done much to increase the autonomy of the University. He had gained a reputation for being open to minority groups in Utah who felt that their views were not adequately represented. This legacy was on Olpin's mind when he said he must not only be open to minority views but also resist the attempts of any pressure group to curb genuine investigation and open expression.

His success in achieving a vigorously independent intellectual climate gained national recognition. In a 1963 article written for *Time* magazine but never published, Utah alumnus Hays Gorey stated, "Few state universities which opened their doors last week could boast of a greater degree of academic freedom, or a more calculatedly burgeoning graduate curriculum than the one hundred and thirteen-year-old institution which claims to be the oldest state university west of the Missouri River."[37]

This was a great change, Gorey pointed out, from the days when the academic atmosphere at the University of Utah had been so stifling that a special committee of distinguished educators—including John Dewey—had come out to investigate

The crowded Dean's Council gathering on Founder's Day in 1950 reflects the rapid academic expansion during the postwar years.

Under the direction of J. R. Mahoney, the Bureau of Economic and Business Research undertook applied regional studies.

In 1946 Dr. Richard Y. Young became the medical school's first full-time dean. He returned to Northwestern University three years later.

Jewish discrimination led hematologist Dr. Maxwell M. Wintrobe to abandon Johns Hopkins University for Utah. He helped build the postwar faculty as head of the College of Medicine.

it. The university had been chastised by the American Association of University Professors in 1915 over undue influence of "the religious denomination to which the majority of the people in the State, and a majority of the Board of Regents adhere—The Church of Jesus Christ of Latter-day Saints, commonly known as the Mormon Church. It was further believed…that the President [Kingsbury] had more than once yielded to this pressure."[38]

Some worried that the new president—a scientist—might neglect the humanities and fine arts. History proved otherwise, and it was Olpin who implemented the idea of a College of Fine Arts. LeRoy J. Robertson, who had just won the Reichhold Award for the outstanding symphonic work in the Western Hemisphere, moved to the University of Utah from Brigham Young University to help fill a void in the preparation of music educators. Maestro Maurice Abravanel received a faculty appointment, and a home was created on campus for the Utah Symphony in 1948.

From securing Fort Douglas to help educate a tripled student body to seeding a cultural renaissance—these were considerable accomplishments, especially amidst the postwar emergency. Those who worked for A. Ray Olpin say it wasn't a strategy so much as an intuitive knack that guided his work. He was driven by a vision of what a university must become to be worthy of being called a university at all. He was determined that the University of Utah should earn the respect he felt was due to it, and he steadfastly went about the work of building that respect.

CHAPTER 3

BATTLING THE WILL OF GOVERNOR LEE

Coping with the campus's rapid growth, particularly the initiative he undertook over Fort Douglas, taught A. Ray Olpin lessons in politics that were put to the test in a very public battle of wills launched by Utah Governor J. Bracken Lee. Lee was a fiscal conservative who was convinced that university administrators, professors, and most of the staff—from the librarians to the janitorial crew—were overpaid and underworked. Time and again he lambasted the "U" for having a maintenance staff of sixty-six employees, directed by twenty-two supervisors.[1] Olpin kept telling Lee that wasn't true and chided him for spreading misinformation. State tax levies for education 25 percent above the national average rankled Lee—especially since Utah was a relatively poor state. He vehemently opposed income tax, and through hefty spending cuts in all of his administrations, he was able to keep budgets in the black.

In 1949 Lee suggested trimming $38 million from state budget requests, with higher education receiving the biggest cut of all. He wanted higher learning's allocation to be practically chopped in half from a requested $10,580,000 to $5,700,000. Olpin asserted that that amount was only sufficient to maintain the University of Utah's operations. Lee wanted the cuts to be spread across Utah Agricultural College in Logan, the University of Utah, Carbon Junior College in Price, Dixie Junior College in St. George, and Weber Junior College in Ogden, plus the branch campuses of the Agricultural College: the College of Southern Utah in Cedar City and Snow College in Ephraim.[2] University boosters weighed

29

Utah Symphony maestro Maurice Abravanel entertains Utah Governor J. Bracken Lee.

in. Dr. Ray E. Spendlove, president of the University of Utah Alumni Association of Uintah County, wrote to Governor Lee that while his "policy of frugality comes like a breath of fresh air to the suffocating,…there are institutions that we hold very dear and feel are worthy of our tax dollar. Our Universities, and in our particular case, the University of Utah, is [sic] such an institution." He explained that taxes for education were an investment, "enabling our children to partake of higher education at its best. Your Excellency, we realize that by one stroke of the pen the efforts of decades can be leveled."[3] He sent the letter by special delivery from Vernal, 275 miles east of Salt Lake City.

Just as the university was celebrating the one-hundredth anniversary of its founding, Lee vetoed $40 million in statewide appropriations, setting the stage for a battle over education spending. In a centenary observance that drew delegates from two hundred educational institutions and almost a hundred learned societies,

Olpin emphasized the school's humble beginnings. He pointed out that in 1852 for "want of funds" teaching had been suspended. He noted that the university had partially reopened as a business school in 1867, but it was not until 1869 that John R. Park was appointed president to reestablish and reorganize what became the University of Utah in 1892. He also noted that reaching a one-hundredth birthday was a milestone not yet achieved by any other state-supported university west of the Missouri River.[4]

While the centennial celebration was planned to show how far the University of Utah had come since its founding, Olpin called attention to the lack of space and alluded to the school's budget woes. He noted that even with the acquisition of 460 acres from Fort Douglas, "the campus today is 100 acres smaller than it was a century ago."[5] With Governor Lee on the dais wearing his first-ever cap and gown, Olpin pointed out "some persons…who feel that Utah's institutions of higher learning are outgrowing the State's ability to support them, what with twice as many students enrolled here for each 1,000 population as in a typical state." He spent the rest of his speech pointing out that teachers had to compete with the modern conveniences of 1950 and propaganda from pressure groups for the chance to shape the minds of young Americans. It was clear that trying circumstances continued to affect the institution, weighing heavily on the mind of its leader.

Lee was unsympathetic. Determined to balance the state's budget, he told Olpin he should "kick out about 2,000 students" and simultaneously raise tuition to nullify the university's Board of Regents' request for increased appropriations the following year.[6] The governor questioned the state's ability to provide positions for university graduates, and he thought that educators, intent on extending their spheres of influence and jobs, were to blame for an overemphasis on academic life. He removed from the Board of Regents five members deemed too sympathetic to the university. One axed regent, businessman Frank Browning of Ogden, determined not to go down without a fight. He even pledged to go into politics himself to expose the harm he felt Lee was causing education. In his reply to Lee, he said,

> Your letter advising me of the reason you have failed to re-appoint me to the Board of Regents of the University of Utah has been received. I admire your frankness to say the least …. Your philosophy of government is so foreign to mine that you have all the reason in the world to pack the Board with men who shall follow your dictates.
>
> During my period there, when I felt the regime of the University was wrong, I was very blunt in my challenge to them, just as I have been with your dictates.
>
> Where we differ is that you, through this mania you have for economy in state government, are going, in my estimation, to leave the State and its institutional physical assets

in a sad state of affairs, and some day the Kennecott lobbyists and all of Wall Street, who arc so profitably depleting our state resources, will tip their hats and abandon their depleted pits, and Utah, with its run-down institutions, will forlornly wonder what its [*sic*] all about.

As a business man, I feel that your caustic approach to the problems of our institutions that the majority of our people hold dear to themselves, will bring down on business a state administration in the future that will make all invested wealth suffer.[7]

The same day that Lee proposed a revamped Board of Regents (with only one incumbent reappointment), the *Salt Lake Tribune* headlined an article detailing a dispute between the university and the governor on enrollment projections, "Lee-Olpin Budgetary 'Tiff' Waxes Anew." Wrote Olpin in his journal, "I am very much disgusted with the whole thing. It seems that the governor is using the tactics of Joe Stalin of Russia, trying to pervert figures and make headlines, and keep those negotiating with him in hot water at all times."[8]

A taxpayers' champion, Lee had been elected to statewide office by an overwhelming majority. He was also Utah's first Republican governor in twenty-four years. Lee came from Price, Utah, and had been an agent for Equitable Insurance. He had enlisted in the army before his high school commencement and had not attended college. He also insisted upon calling President Olpin "Doc."[9]

Despite pride in all his accomplishments, Olpin threatened to resign and let Brack Lee run the university. Lee said that if Olpin's interest in good government was evidenced by holding out for a big appropriation, that might be a good thing, too.[10] Under Olpin's leadership, the campus had become less like a liberal-arts college and more like a regional university. It had expanded to accommodate the influx of veterans returning from the war. Assembling and implementing a greatly enlarged faculty—first through employing some part-time and temporary personnel, then by adding ranking staff—had necessitated the appointment of a dean of the faculty. The mandatory student counseling under the GI Bill required the establishment of a guidance center and appointment of a dean of students. The amplified demands for graduate training called for the expansion of the graduate division into a graduate school, with its new dean. The doctor-of-philosophy degree came to be offered in almost every field of learning, and more than a hundred students were studying for doctoral degrees.

Among the new academic and professional schools established were the College of Mines and Mineral Industries, the College of Fine Arts, the College of Pharmacy, and the College of Nursing. Within existing colleges, new departments had been created with staff interested in better administration and teaching. An

Members of the 1948 University of Utah Board of Regents helped dull the axe of budget-cutting Governor J. Bracken Lee.

Institute of World Affairs and an Institute of Government were organized to facilitate an understanding of world problems and train students for government service. The College of Arts and Sciences and the lower division courses were merged into a university college, charged with the responsibility of directing the general-education program. To expedite and more efficiently handle matters requiring faculty attention, the Faculty Council, composed of elected representatives from various academic areas, was established. This council constituted the educational policy making body of the university, reviewing all resignations, appointments, and promotions of the faculty. A director was hired to supervise the operation of buildings, now consisting of many temporary, wooden structures as well as permanent ones, and the campus auxiliaries.

Regardless of this growth and improvement, once the veterans graduated and the federal financial aid stopped flowing in, Lee expected the university budget to decline. Olpin felt this viewpoint was wholly undemocratic. He saw education as an economically equalizing force and the only one capable of preparing an educated citizenry competent to salve the war's worldwide wounds. He expressed his philosophy of education in a speech to the Salt Lake Advertising Club:

There is no question but that a university must serve the economic needs of the state which supports it and the clientele which attends it, but in a democracy the citizenry has a much higher stake in the success of its educational institutions. As Jefferson remarked, nothing is more important, nothing more legitimate, than that of rendering the people safe-guardians of their own liberty. It was Jefferson's conviction that an enlightened electorate is the one chief hope of our democracy. The influence of a government in a democracy must be shared among all the people, in consequence education must be shared among all the people....

Part of the reason America is at such a loss as to what is the appropriate foreign policy in the United States is to be traced to the fact that we have rested the obligation and responsibility of our government upon all our people, including the tradesman, but have assumed that the tradesman need not share in the knowledge of the social sciences and history, which are the foundations upon which a rational judgment of our national action must be based.

It is also true that the trend of modern industry is such that every tradesman will not have leisure time enough to reflect upon his obligation as a citizen, if we school him in the habit and methods of wise reflection. Apart from the need to train every citizen to play his role well as a democratic statesman, there remains the fact that the increase of leisure time, incident to the development of modern industrial methods, has not been paralleled by any appreciable increase in the capacity of the American man to use his leisure time wisely.[11]

Praise for the virtues of liberal education held no sway with Governor Lee. He demanded that cuts be implemented. On April 21, 1951, he threw down the gauntlet when he directed the university to conduct a department-by-department personnel audit. He wanted a table showing the breakdown of employees from instructional staff to the maintenance force. He wanted the inventory to include the number of employees, their positions and duties, and their average salaries. If any employees received additional salary from other than state sources, such information should be noted and included. "This information," he wrote, "will be of considerable value to the Legislature, so I will appreciate receiving it in ample time to present to the forthcoming special session I am planning to call." The date of the legislative special session was set for the University of Utah's commencement day—June 4.[12]

Board of Regents Chair Sterling Sill also received a letter that day from Governor Lee. After noting that universities in the East were trimming staffs to work within their budgets, Lee stated that when standing armies are reduced, the staff must also decrease. Then he forecast layoffs: "I am going to recommend to the legislature that the appropriations for higher education be somewhat reduced from the present figure. Such reduction, undoubtedly, will require that certain State institutions, if not all of them, will have to make appropriate reductions among their employees. Under these circumstances, I believe it would be wise and just to notify those employees most likely to be released so that they can attempt to seek other employment."[13]

Olpin bristled at the idea of Lee being so controlling. He said there was no way that he could furnish the information requested within such a short period of time. He explained to the governor that the university had already given most of the data to the State Finance Commission, where it was available for review. "If it is not, we repeat that we shall be pleased to furnish that which is lacking as soon as the Secretary's Office can be relieved from the mass of details associated with the regular Commencement program," he wrote.[14] Record checking and diploma preparation made this the busiest month of the year at the university, he reminded the governor. With this letter, he included copies of the "Financial Report of the Secretary and Controller" and the *Report of the President.*

In fact, the postwar enrollment at the "U" had peaked in 1948–49, the school year when it was decided there were too many graduates to file by President Olpin at commencement. U.S. colleges and universities experienced a 7.4 percent decline in enrollment in 1950 as veteran registrations dropped and the Korean War crisis ensued. Enrollment losses were attributed to the draft, exhaustion of World War II benefits by veterans, and uncertainty about whether students would be allowed to complete their collegiate careers during the Korean conflict.[15] By 1951 veterans still made up one-third of the University of Utah's student body.

One of the contentions that Governor Lee and State Finance Commissioner Patrick H. Mulcahy made was that students registering for less than ten hours' credit should be excluded from the student head counts that determined how much money was allocated under the basic budget formula. Olpin and the university's Board of Regents were already irritated by the finance commissioner's "attempt to usurp powers delegated to the Regents under the Constitution."[16] A statute enacted just before the war had created the Finance Commission to administer the budgets of state departments and agencies. The commission had previously requested the names of all members of the university staff who were paid more than $375 per month and the amounts they received.[17]

Lee was determined to veto the university's request for dedicated credits plus the amount the legislature had recommended as an increased appropriation. In a meeting at the governor's office on March 6, 1951, Olpin asked for reconsideration. In his journal, Olpin described the grueling session as one of the most exhausting of his career: "Lee loosed a tirade against education and especially against the University for its selfishness. He began to shout so loud that I am sure he could have been heard a half mile away if a window had been open. He accused us of trying to wreck the State, of being greedy. He called me a hog, trying to get away with more than our share…The whole thing started when I tried to explain to him why we had a growing number of part-time students."[18]

The meeting lasted an hour and a half. "My nerve patterns," Olpin noted in his journal, "were almost exhausted, I had dancing jitters and a numb right hand. It was nothing that I had said, it was just what I had had to listen to."[19] Also in the meeting were Board of Regents Chair William O'Connor and the governor's secretary, Harold W. Simpson. The following day Lee sent Olpin a terse letter expressing regret that "our discussion yesterday was at times unpleasant."[20] He also told Olpin that he felt the session had helped each of them arrive at some common ground which should assure better relations in the future. Olpin sent a curt reply, stating that "even though some unpleasantries seemed to develop at the time of my recent visit to your office, I am sure the discussions ended with both of us having a better understanding of our objectives. I trust that we can work harmoniously together to achieve them."[21]

Apostle Joseph F. Merrill wrote a private letter on LDS Church stationery to Lee on June 6, 1951, detailing his views and supporting Lee's action. Merrill believed that the state institutions of higher learning were already spending more money than was necessary to educate effectively. He praised former University of Utah President George Thomas but criticized Olpin for his ambitious desire to make the school one of the country's outstanding universities. He thought that it was economically impossible for Utah to gratify Olpin's ambition. Merrill insisted that there were a far greater number of courses offered in the state universities than were necessary to meet the requirements of 98 percent of the students. It was, he said, unreasonable to ask economically small Utah to do what Harvard, Chicago, Columbia, and other great universities were doing.[22]

In the end, Utah legislators aligned against Lee and his attacks on Utah's institutions of higher learning. "Record appropriations were made to these schools two years ago when enrollment was high and the facilities crowded. Since then there has been a decline in enrollment, but the requests for appropriations have continued to increase," the governor lamented.[23] Lee then requested a ten-thousand-dollar appropriation to contract with an efficiency firm to conduct a job evaluation at the university; it was voted down. The day before the start of the special legislative session, Lee and Olpin were on the podium together again—this time in the stadium at the annual spring commencement. University officials hadn't expected Lee to attend. They hastily rearranged the stage to make room for him and gave the governor a cap and gown to wear.

The legislative special session that Lee convened from June 4 through 16, 1951, enacted an amendment to the state appropriations act, earmarking for the University of Utah $5,149,475 from the state's general fund.[24] After threatening another veto, Lee permitted the supplemental appropriation bill to become law. The caveat, he wrote to the Board of Regents chair, was that he would not approve future quarterly allotments to the University of Utah and Utah Agricultural College until he received a satisfactory job evaluation from each institution. To his job-audit request of two months earlier, he piled on analysis of the curriculum of the institution, including the courses taught, average number of students in each course, and any special costs involved. Then Lee determined that the scope of the survey should not be prescribed: "In fact, I believe it would be desirable to go into any and all aspects of our higher education problems, and I encourage the Board to follow that procedure," he wrote.[25] Moreover, he suggested that the two universities cooperate to employ an outside firm of efficiency experts to conduct the reviews.

What had begun as a vague charge of mismanagement grew into a thorough shakedown. Superintendent of Public Instruction E. Allen Bateman called the ten-thousand-dollar job-evaluation study of Utah's institutions of higher learning an attempt at dictatorship by Governor Lee. The volunteers serving as regents construed Lee's actions as votes of no confidence for his board appointees. Sterling Sill, who was turning the mantle of leadership over to William O'Connor, announced that the Board of Regents had filed a lawsuit over what members considered a constitutional infringement of its rights and duties to govern.[26] Harold W. Simpson, Lee's assistant, issued a press release stating that the job evaluation had first been proposed by a faculty member at one of the institutions who said researchers were freeloaders. The governor's communiqué said, "Institutions and departments which have established certain routines frequently are unable to visualize efficiency and economy reforms that can be detected very easily by experts trained to look for such things."[27] Publication of the release caused Olpin further embarrassment.

One aspect of Olpin's efficiency that was scrutinized was his ability to carry out all the pressing duties of the day. According to his assistant, Paul Hodson, who had also been assistant to President LeRoy Cowles, the Board of Regents urged more delegation and faster action on Olpin's part. Although Olpin and Hodson worked together over the course of Olpin's entire administration and functioned well as colleagues, Hodson wrote that crucial presidential decisions got backlogged on Olpin's fifteen-foot-long table, which was stacked high with unorganized mail and papers. Hodson "tried to develop a system of check sheets so that Olpin could look at a letter and check it, but it never worked with him. He would hold them."[28]

Hodson wrote a rather heavy-handed memo about systematization of work in the president's office where he noted that "mail taken to the President's desk is frequently handled a half dozen times or more before it is actually taken care of. Sometimes it is never taken care of. Bad public relations result."[29]

Olpin had appealed previously to the Board of Regents, requesting permission to add staff to aid him in administering his rapidly growing responsibilities. Hodson echoed his frustration, "He [Olpin] had very little staff; and despite the degree of autonomy we had, President Olpin was responsible for making more decisions in more areas than was humanly possible. Aside from me, he had hired Jacob Geerlings as dean of the faculty and Parry D. Sorensen as chief of the new Public Relations Department. We three and the clerical staff constituted administration in the president's office."[30]

Other key personnel at that time included G. Homer Durham, who directed the Institute of Government, a training service and research unit in the field of governmental activities and problems; and Harold W. Bentley, head of the University of Utah Press, dean of the summer school, director of the Humanities Foundation, and professor of English.

Still, the Board of Regents saw as politically impractical the proposed organizational and structural changes that Olpin felt were necessary to conserve his time and energy for the most important matters. They looked positively on the management survey Lee was demanding. A proper survey by a reputable firm, they hoped, might yield results complimentary to the university, improving its public image.[31] Knowing such a study could have a drastic effect on his reputation, Olpin detailed in his journal some of the cautions he raised with the Board of Regents on July 2, 1951. "I had pointed out the dangers of a study by efficiency experts of curricula and how Huey Long had built a large campus with beautiful buildings at Louisiana State University, but that Louisiana State University had lost its accreditation because of interference by the Governor in the subjects being taught. It was decided that they would not look into the curriculum problems at the present time."[32]

The Board of Regents discussed a survey of Columbia University that had been conducted by a national management and consulting firm, Booz, Allen, and Hamilton. O'Connor agreed to head the search for consultants, and Booz, Allen, and Hamilton's firm was hired to "appraise the effectiveness with which University funds are being utilized"[33] with the University of Utah footing the bill, which rose to more than twenty-five thousand dollars. A balance in the university's contingency fund was tapped to pay the cost.

Siding with Olpin, the Board of Regents agreed that many of the issues Lee had raised about the university's academic operations should remain outside the consultants' purview. A letter to O'Connor from Stewart M. Lowry of the national firm's San Francisco office detailed this prearrangement:

> The degrees granted, the curricula, their academic content and teaching techniques are to be accepted as they presently exist. The survey is to be concerned with their cost.
>
> The principal element of cost is the salaries paid to people. The survey would therefore examine the adequacy of the organization of the university, the numbers of people required to man it, the effectiveness of their utilization, and the salaries paid to them. The report will contain recommendations in those areas in which we found opportunities for improvement.[34]

Before the consultants arrived, presidential assistant Hodson rehearsed with Olpin the advantages and disadvantages of full cooperation. Should the university adopt a "stand-offish" attitude toward this, "the governor's survey?" Hodson noted that the staff would need to be sold on the benefits of the survey—to receive authentic encouragement from the central administration. Otherwise, he speculated, the staff was quite apt to be negative. To protect Olpin from being blindsided by problems that might be raised in interviews with the consultants, Hodson recommended that key groups such as the physical-plant operators, the Equipment Control Cabinet, and the Deans' Council be invited to submit preliminary problems to the central administration. This, he said, would give the president the advantage of being informed about the issues in advance.[35]

The consultants arrived, and the study commenced on April 7, 1952. Olpin had considerable influence on the report, which was issued to the university's Board of Regents six months later. With stubborn pride, he received the consultants' recommendation that two vice presidents be added to the university's administration. Olpin had twenty-seven people reporting to him; the consultants recommended reducing them to six. In the new proposed organization, one vice president would oversee academics, and another act as business manager.

The 153-page report was bound in black, simulated reptile skin and embossed with gold lettering, and copies were widely distributed. The consultants found "little evidence of extravagance" in historical or current university expenditures, which Olpin also found gratifying.[36] A predicted downward trend in enrollment with a recommended cut of $800,000 in expenditures for 1954 to 1958 did give him cause to quarrel. "The report has much to commend it," he said, but he declared it would be "impossible without lowering the standing of the school to reduce the budget by $800,000 a biennium."[37] Olpin also felt certain that Utah's population growth and college demand would exceed predictions.

Handwritten responses to specific points in the report on the president's personal stationery reveal Olpin's slightly bruised ego:

> Could not reorganization plan be presented just as effectively without first accusing president of creating bad organization because of unwillingness to delegate authority?

> This is small reward for willingness to work hard in face of public criticism of too much administrative help.

> Similarly unwarranted criticism of president for not opening doors of his office to everyone does not quite jibe with actual experience of comments. Pile of paper on desk reflect amount of time in personal interviews. Most frequent comment I hear is about my willingness to see anyone and attend everything.[38]

The Board of Regents issued a politically motivated statement in response to the report: "The Board plans to move slowly in order to evaluate these recommendations. It recognizes that in some particulars the point of view of business consultants trained to think in terms of cost reduction may be at variance with the purposes of higher education, which is designed to fulfill a purpose of greater enlightenment in a world whose survival is at the crossroads of democracy versus communism."[39]

But, as a result of the administrative survey, the first two vice presidents in the history of the University of Utah were appointed, and top Park Building aides were exactly what Olpin had been urging since 1946. The Board of Regents established the vice presidencies on February 9, 1953—some seven months after it had received the report. Elmo R. Morgan, former field manager of the Atomic Energy Commission in Los Alamos, New Mexico, and coordinator of cooperative research at the University of Utah since 1951, was appointed business vice president. G. Homer Durham, who had headed the Institute of Government since 1946 and the Department of Political Science since 1948, was named academic vice president. Olpin was finally able to acquire two key executives to aid him in the university's administration.

Enrollment did begin to fall comparatively rapidly in the 1952–53 school year as the veterans graduated. This decline reached its lowest point during the next school year with an enrollment of 7,142 students. Although this enrollment was the lowest of the decade, it was still substantially higher than any of the prewar years. Olpin made a persuasive argument that costs per student had risen with the increasing specialization of the faculty, growing maintenance costs resulting from the acquisition of a hundred buildings and 298 acres of land from Fort Douglas, and the number of university students in graduate school who had to be taught

Business Vice President Elmo Morgan brought critical expertise in research administration to the university from his stint at the atomic-bomb project at Los Alamos.

Political scientist G. Homer Durham was the University of Utah's first academic vice president. Later, he became the tenth president of Arizona State University.

by high-salaried experts. "Education," he wrote in his journal, "is not just a pat of butter which, if spread over only one slice of bread, may be twice as thick as if shared by two."[40] The administration noted the following obstacles to reducing per-student costs:

1. If enrollment decreased back to the 1939-40 level,

2. If the size of the plant were reduced to the size it was then,

3. If we went back to a strictly undergraduate level,

4. If the student-per-teacher ratio were reestablished at the old level,

5. Then, costs (adjusted for the change in the price level) would go back to the older per-student cost figure.[41]

Coincident with the problems of financing and organizing higher education to meet America's postwar needs was a growing concern over the political lives and views of university professors. The Un-American Activities Committee of the U.S. House of Representatives sent Olpin a letter requesting a list of textbooks and supplementary reading material in use at the University of Utah. Universities were to give the committee the names of authors and titles of textbooks for courses in sociology, geography, economics, government, philosophy, history, political science, and American literature.[42] This audit of course materials, committee chair John S.

Wood wrote in a supplementary explanation, was the result of serious allegations made in a lengthy petition filed by the National Sons of the American Revolution. The request, he wrote, "should not be construed as having the slightest unfavorable reflection or criticism upon your school or any person connected therewith."[43]

The action caught Olpin, who had been so involved in assembling university research to benefit the nation's defense, by surprise. From the day that he arrived in Salt Lake City to head the university, he had been stumping for humane education that would teach students the responsibilities of leadership and democracy in the atomic age. While Olpin was considering how to respond to the inquiry, the National Education Association weighed in with a letter calling the examination of college texts for Communist propaganda a "dangerous procedure and threat to academic freedom."[44] Olpin told the Board of Regents he shared the education organization's resentment.

Yet Olpin, in turn, ignited a Red Scare at the University of Utah, giving Lee another cause to withhold funds, when it was reported in June of 1949 that he strongly suspected that a member of the faculty was an organizer for the Communist Party. Olpin revealed that if the individual in question received a one-year extension of his contract, the professor would become tenured—entitled to hold his position at the university indefinitely. The Board of Regents began discussing issuing a ban on Communists at the University of Utah and also requiring faculty members to sign pledges of loyalty to the United States. Publicly, the president entrusted judgment to the Faculty Council Committee on Academic Freedom and Tenure, although he recommended that the Board of Regents hear the case first. He charged the faculty committee with crafting a public-position statement on the rights and responsibilities of faculty members as citizens. He also assigned the committee the case of Dr. James Toman, assistant professor of physiology in the College of Medicine.

Olpin told the committee, "Various accusations of Communist activity had been received by the administration, and the Board of Regents had discussed the problem. Dr. Toman, state chairman of the Progressive Party and active in several controversies over teachers' contracts in local schools, would, under existing University regulations, achieve tenure if employed after December 12, 1949. The Board, being uncertain as to the wisdom of re-employing Dr. Toman, had offered him a modified contract while considering the issue of tenure."[45]

The modified contract included notice of the university's right to terminate it. Toman signed under protest, appealing to Olpin to conduct a full investigation. Toman requested that his case be reviewed by the Faculty Council Committee on Academic Freedom and Tenure on the premise that the extraordinary stipulation

Olpin strongly suspected that Assistant Professor of Physiology James E. P. Toman was a communist. Toman was forced to leave his university teaching job in 1949.

from the Board of Regents "was based upon a consideration of the presumed political beliefs of the employee and upon his participation in the political life of the community."[46]

In an appeal to the Faculty Council Committee the following day, Toman noted that he felt it "my duty as a teacher and scientist and as an American citizen to challenge those who would limit our academic freedom and constitutional liberties,"[47] and that no charges had been brought against him. What about the state law that "no political or religious test shall be required or partiality or preference shown in the appointment of professors?"[48]

Professor Toman's colleagues and supervisors attested to his sterling academic performance.[49] Some pointed out that he was innocent until proven guilty; "that he should be given the opportunity to know the charges and their source, and to meet and answer his accusers."[50]

The Board of Regents met with Olpin in executive session. They decided to extend Toman's contract month to month until an investigation by the Faculty Council Committee could make recommendations to the Faculty Board for a policy concerning teachers allegedly connected with subversive activities.[51] O. Meredith Wilson, dean of the College of Arts and Sciences, drafted a statement on the rights and responsibilities of university teachers to be written into the faculty code. It said that teachers should not be expected to surrender their liberties or give up their rights to participate in public life, including influencing the formulation of public opinion. It also stressed teachers' responsibility to exercise the restraint appropriate to the dignity of the learned profession.[52] Its adoption by the Faculty Council Committee was intended to forestall off-campus action to require a loyalty oath and help with a more immediate personnel problem, Wilson wrote.[53] While Professor Toman awaited his chance to appeal, a security guard at his laboratory kept tabs on his comings and goings, sending detailed reports to Olpin.

The Faculty Council Committee determined there was no justifiable reason to terminate Toman's employment; he never was called to testify. A note written on Olpin's copy of the minutes said that twenty days after the committee met, he had its findings changed to state that the committee had insufficient information to decide *whether or not* a contract should be offered.[54] According to the night-watchman's allegations, Toman had suspicious visitors coming and going into his office on weekends and at night and a questionable relationship with an unmarried woman graduate student working in his lab. Olpin brought all this information to the university's Board of Regents. A motion was made not to hire Toman for the coming year and to terminate his contract on December 1. This was Olpin's comment:

> I want to make it clear in the record. The only thing I would take a definite stand on personally—I have left this up to the Faculty and the Board and I haven't taken a stand on anything like freedom; that a person could express as he wants, but I cannot as administrator of this University condone things he has been doing over the weekend, let alone the things that have been going on over a period of time. If the man does that what difference does it make if he has tenure or not? It isn't a question in my mind of anything except his fitness to be a faculty member, that is, his moral conduct.[55]

The motion passed, with Regent George S. Ballif dissenting over trying a man in absentia "for Communism," "using totalitarian methods."[56] At the same meeting, Olpin asked for guidance on whether he was authorized to negotiate with a labor union that had gained power on campus. This was the nonacademic employees' union, the United Public Workers of America. The Board of Regents directed him not to bargain with members of the union.

Olpin was called to task by the School of Medicine's executive committee members for the role he had played in ousting Toman. Olpin's actions, they said, raised serious questions in their minds regarding administrative policies. "Even in a situation where questions of indiscretion are involved, it is our opinion that the individual should be allowed to state his case before the deciding group, although the evidence may appear to be conclusive against him."[57] Its members objected that the professor had been dismissed without justification and that the Board of Regents had made the decision without consulting his department head. Speaking for the executive committee were doctors Emil G. Holmstrom and Max Wintrobe. Doctors Louis S. Goodman and Horace Davenport asked the board to reconsider its action.

By this point, Olpin was on his way to Sao Paulo, Brazil, with sixteen members of the Ute basketball squad. The team had been invited to play ten exhibition games on an expense-paid trip celebrating the tenth anniversary of the Floresta amateur sports association. The head of the LDS Church's mission in Sao Paulo, Rulon S. Howells, had urged Olpin to accompany the team on the tour, which included games in Rio de Janeiro, and made arrangements for pro-Utah publicity in the Brazilian newspapers. "There is a great deal of good that can be done both for the team and Inter-American relations with the educational leaders here in Brasil,"

Howells wrote in one of several letters to Olpin between August and October of that year.[58]

With inner-American problems between scholars and politicians occupying nearly all of his time, Olpin opted to join the team on the two-week tour. Hodson kept him updated on developments in the Toman situation by telegram. Regent Sterling Sill wanted the Board of Regents' executive committee to meet to extend Professor Toman's contract six more months, until the end of the academic year on June 30.[59] No action was taken.

Dr. James E.P. Toman resigned his position on November 18, 1949. He left Utah for Chicago and went on to a distinguished career in the chemical modulation of brain function.[60] Throughout the rest of his presidency, in speeches on academic freedom and responsibility, Olpin championed diversity of views and an atmosphere conducive to their expression at the University of Utah.

CHAPTER 4

SETTING SIGHTS ON WASHINGTON

The Second World War intensified government's need for both basic and applied research, bridging the gap between experimental and theoretical physics, research that Olpin had done during and after college. When its program director died unexpectedly, Olpin was placed in charge of the entire war-research program at one of the country's most research-intensive universities: Ohio State. His career blossomed with this unanticipated turn of events. Olpin was transformed from a technical expert on the transmission of sound, light, and electrical waves into an administrator whose job was convincing government and industry leaders to let universities help solve the world's most threatening problems.

Under his direction, the Ohio State University's research facilities were instrumental in developing projects important to the war effort—and beyond. For example, the experiments of a psychology professor, together with technological devices developed by the research laboratories, were incorporated into a recognition training program that enabled a person to learn to distinguish, in a fraction of a second, between American and enemy planes and ships. The problem of recognizing aircraft had proved so baffling during the war that "there were many instances where military security necessitated the shooting down of every plane, friend or foe, seen in the air. It was that important that no enemy plane be allowed to slip through." Military personnel from throughout the country were sent to Columbus to learn to distinguish between airplanes using this "Renshaw system."[1]

Other investigations initiated by the Ohio State research program included designing radar antennae and creating high-octane gasoline for war planes and experimenting with synthetic rubber, mildew proofing, welding, and metal hardening—literally everything from explosives to antibiotics. Ohio State was also under contract to the Manhattan Project. Most of the work was classified, and the two hundred Ohio State researchers working on the government-research program under the auspices of the Research Foundation took its classified status very seriously.

Olpin was in charge of maintaining this veil of secrecy, acting as liaison between Columbus and Washington.[2] He began to see that when research was paid for wholly or partly by commercial firms or federal or state agencies, it had a profound effect on the amount and variety of research that could be carried on by graduate students and faculty members. He delineated the following three objectives for this work: "first, creating and improving combat devices to win the war; second, creating substitutes for scarce materials; third, developing means of cushioning the shock of post-war adjustment."[3] His duties to further those ends included working with principal investigators and department heads to manage contracts and patents.[4] He frequently predicted that advancements in basic research were the key to winning the war, noting that "Hitler has lessened his ultimate chances by driving theoretical scientists from Germany and putting those remaining to 'gadgeteering.'"[5] Cooperative research, Olpin felt, was the genius of America.

It seemed he even loved the modernizing capabilities of television. But in preaching the virtues of universities conducting industrial research, A. Ray Olpin discovered his true calling. He found his work at Ohio State more interesting and satisfying than any he had done before.[6] One of the statements he was fond of quoting came from Harold Deforest Arnold, the director of research at Bell Telephone Laboratories, his former employer: "Research is the effort of the mind to comprehend relationships which no one has previously known. And in its finest exemplifications it is practical as well as theoretical; trending always toward worthwhile relationships; demanding common sense as well as uncommon ability."[7]

During his eight years at the Ohio State University Research Foundation, the annual income from nonstate sources for project research increased from $56,000 to approximately $2.5 million. Toward the end of the war, many of the research projects Olpin had been involved in were declassified. Various groups around the country were fascinated with the peacetime applications of wartime research. In the spring of 1945, he received an invitation to speak in Utah at the Ogden Rotary Club's annual Ladies' Night dinner. Roy D. Thatcher, then chairman of the

University of Utah's Board of Regents, was a member of the Ogden club, and other members of the board were also in attendance.

Some members of the Board of Regents already knew Olpin because he had been a minor candidate for the University of Utah's presidency in 1941 when LeRoy Cowles had been appointed. This time around, regents were anxious to close the deal: they had heard rumors from Olpin's cousin that A. Ray had forestalled taking a thirty-thousand-dollar job in New York City while he waited to hear about the president's job at Utah. He also had been considered for the presidency of both Brigham Young University and Utah Agricultural College in Logan.[8]

When Olpin traveled to Utah in July 1945 for his Ogden speaking engagement, he was met at the Union Pacific train station by Thatcher and others, who took him to the University Club in Salt Lake City. He was being rushed. These volunteers represented a search committee seeking candidates for the position of president of the University of Utah. James Wade, who chaired the search, had heard of Olpin's work from Stewart Zimmerley of the U.S. Bureau of Mines. Zimmerley had met Olpin at a conference where he had spoken. The search committee arranged for Olpin to meet with and address the Board of Regents on July 13, 1945.

Although Olpin was, at the time, busy completing reports on classified projects at Ohio State, his keen interest in the University of Utah and awareness of its problems were evident in a letter he wrote to President Cowles on May 31, 1945. Cowles had requested information from Olpin about the Research Foundation at Ohio State. In his reply, Olpin wrote,

> It is my firm belief that money should be obtained from industry for the support of a comprehensive research program in Salt Lake City. I think such a program could open the doors to the many promising Utah boys and girls who are now locating in other sections of the country. I believe that a research foundation in connection with the University would pave the way for the development of an outstanding graduate school there. I believe that you and I are in agreement in this matter and I hope that we may work together to see our hopes develop into something of value to the University and the people in that region.[9]

Cowles's own nomination to the president's position had been the result of a tie vote by the regents for two other candidates: Adam S. Bennion of Utah Power and Light, a former commissioner of education for the Mormon Church, and Lowry Nelson, a liberal Mormon sociologist and professor at the University of Minnesota. Two rounds of votes had ended with ties: seven each for Bennion and Nelson. It had become clear that the board would be unable to produce a majority vote for either candidate, so Regent W. H. Leigh made the motion to add to the ballot the name of LeRoy E. Cowles, the newly appointed dean of the School of Education. Cowles was nominated president just four years before his anticipated retirement. His appointment as the sixth president to lead the University of Utah was considered an interim one.[10]

When Cowles reached the set retirement age in April 1945, the Board of Regents reactivated the presidential search committee. Its members included Wade, Thatcher, and Mrs. Dan B. Shields, A. H. Reiser, Thornton D. Morris, and President Cowles as an ex officio member. The board also appointed a faculty search committee consisting of Dean William H. Leary, Dean E. E. Erickson, Dr. Orin Tugman, Professor R. S. Lewis, and Dean Sidney W. Angleman.

When the regents met with Olpin in July, they knew that members of the Utah press were eager to hear of any decisions that related to selecting Cowles's successor. Therefore, they pressed Olpin to allow them to announce his candidacy. Olpin gave his permission; however, he felt that he should notify his superiors in Ohio before saying that he would accept the job if he received a definite offer. Even before Olpin had left Utah, newspaper articles appeared, announcing his candidacy.

When he arrived in Columbus, his wife, Elva, met him with an Ohio newspaper that had also published an article about his candidacy. She was understandably eager to hear more from the candidate himself. Elva was particularly anxious to return home to Utah.

At the Board of Regents meeting on July 27, 1945, Regent Wade presented information that he had collected about Olpin, reading letters of recommendation and citing the candidate's credentials. All the members of the board were favorably impressed. However, despite Olpin's advocacy of basic research as an integral part of the scholarly activity of faculty and graduate students, members of the faculty search committee were concerned about his inexperience with administration of an academic institution and felt they needed more information before approving his selection. They sent Olpin a letter requesting his position on the following:

1. the most significant immediate problems confronting the state and the university;

2. the function of the faculty in university government, especially the place of faculty advisory councils such as the Administrative Council at the University of Utah;

3. Areas of development and emphasis in the future policy of the University with special reference to the position of the liberal arts and sciences.[11]

Olpin's reply to the faculty request was a five-page statement that revealed both his perception of the problems that the university faced within the state and his concern and support for liberal education. He said that Utah could not afford to continue shipping out raw materials for processing and then buying them back, fabricated, for much more than had been spent in mining them. He mentioned the problem of fitting returning veterans into the educational system, and he said that all students should be trained for world citizenship. He also said that a state university must provide technical assistance for the industries of the state and at the same time offer a liberal education, including "those things of cultural value." Furthermore, he wrote,

> In order that they may be happy and contented in their new environment students should be well trained in the humanities and the arts. They should have basic training in the fundamentals of science philosophy and the arts; should be taught to express themselves competently through various media; should have an understanding of current events; should learn to commune and live effectively with others and to assume and perform the responsibilities of citizenship. At the same time, they should have opportunities to acquire mastery or proficiency in such chosen fields as will enable them to earn their livelihood while making contributions to society.[12]

He also wrote that the faculty should be involved in academic decisions, but he declined to answer the second question directly until he knew more about how the administrative council at the university operated.

Some members of the faculty expressed concern about Olpin's relative lack of teaching experience. They feared that he would be unfamiliar with such details as credits, admissions, grading, student behavior, and curricula. Others were worried about his professional experience as an applied scientist. They suspected that Olpin might neglect the humanities and arts or be insensitive to the major social problems in government and industry confronting the American people. He seemed to them authoritative but not congenial.

Recommendations helped to alleviate most of the faculty committee's concerns. Howard L. Bevis, then president of Ohio State University, praised Olpin for his breadth of understanding of university subject matter and his belief in a liberal education.[13] It was Bevis who had appointed Olpin to chair a subcommittee on research for the Committee on Emergency Cooperation with State and Federal Governments and act as official representative of Ohio State University in defense research contracts.[14] He apparently remained an Olpin fan. Louis Raths, professor of education at Ohio State and an associate of the Ohio State Research Foundation, wrote the faculty committee members that they need have no fears concerning

Olpin's understanding of broad social, economic, and political problems, nor doubt his interest in liberal education.[15] In his letter, Department of Mine Engineering Chair Harry Nold said, "Dr. Olpin's outstanding characteristic is his ability to organize, combined with his ability to get things done and to develop cooperation with himself and among the people who are working on research projects."[16]

Harlan Hatcher, dean of Ohio State's College of Arts and Sciences, wrote of the advantages of "Dr. Olpin's contacts with the leading people in science and industry throughout the country which have led to the placing with our Foundation research projects of very considerable number and importance."[17] Raths, however, was less enthusiastic and expressed some reservations: "The only question which I personally would raise relates to the possibility that he would have much more in common with industrial executives than he would with the common people of Utah."[18]

Members of the faculty committee may well have been insulted by his comment about the commoners of Utah. Raths had also undertaken an Olpin character study and noted, "So far as I could find out, Dr. Olpin does not carry his Mormonism to the point where it would take precedence over other values. In fact, there were a number of his acquaintances who did not know that he was affiliated with the Mormon Church."[19]

The report of the faculty search committee to the regents expressed the opinion that Olpin "was accorded high tributes with respect to his ability as an administrator, his public relations activities, his scientific accomplishments, and his standing in the city in which he resides."[20] Those regents who had heard Olpin speak, or who had met and spoken with him, also shared their positive impressions. The Board of Regents' search committee had also sought opinions from local people of standing who knew Olpin, including Brigham Young University President Franklin Harris. The Board of Regents was in favor of Olpin: he had been responsible for one of the really important research departments during the war. The members felt he had both the personal qualifications and professional status that made him seem ideally suited for the job.

While the regents reviewed the fine points, the Utah media speculated about who the new president would be. Arthur Gaeth, a commentator for Intermountain Network radio, broadcast a long editorial about the kind of man the University of Utah's next president should be: He should be thoroughly acquainted with the Humanities.... He should have a scientific approach. He should be a student of the modern political, economic, and social changes. He should be a war veteran "or know the problems of youth coming out of conflict," Gaeth urged. The favored man should have spiritual insight. He should be a firm believer in the democratic processes and economic freedom. "If he is living in the past, hide-bound by tradition, he will create, by his selections, a conservative institution that will keep Utahns tied to provincialism," the commentator warned. "What a golden opportunity for a man who can read the signs of the times and wield his influence to help an area adjust to them."[21]

The length and focus of the broadcast underscored popular interest in the university presidential selection; the broadcaster's preferred characteristics suited Olpin to a "t." Olpin had given his own radio talk three years earlier. It was titled "Research Wins Wars and Assures Peace."[22]

The top candidate told the regents that he would accept the job, if it was offered, under certain conditions. First, he insisted upon a unanimous vote of support from the board and a free hand in selecting new faculty and developing the curriculum. He also said that consideration should be given to a state-owned president's residence. On August 10, 1945, the regents met to vote on the candidates. Sterling Sill moved the appointment of A. Ray Olpin. Regent Wade told the group that they needed to act quickly because he had been told of other lucrative and prestigious jobs that Olpin was considering. However, since some of the board's members were absent, they adjourned, reconvening that evening at seven thirty. The first item of business was a motion, unanimously approved, to offer Olpin the job. Then, for the record, the committee members made a ballot that included the following names: Willis W. Ritter, John T. Wahlquist, Sidney Angleman, Arthur Beeley, and O. Meredith Wilson. All were faculty men, and none were truly considered for candidacy. That night Olpin was elected at a salary of eleven thousand dollars a year with the appointment starting on July 1, 1946, when President Cowles's term ended. Olpin accepted.[23]

At Olpin's first meeting with the board, the regents proposed that due to President Cowles's poor health and a management crisis in the medical school, which was operating without a dean, the new president should take office on January 1, 1946. Olpin agreed to do so.[24] He advised President Bevis that he would have to wrap up his business at Ohio State six months sooner than he had planned. Even before he left Columbus, Olpin corresponded extensively with President Cowles about salaries he could offer candidates and obtaining surplus equipment from the federal government, particularly from Fort Douglas and the Defense Depot Ogden. From shepherding resources wrought by the atomic age and bestowed upon higher education, to visualizing the transitions required to build a peacetime economy, Olpin synthesized his experiences and brought to Utah a dedication to leveraging the federal government's largesse. Utah officials had been very good at promoting the state's location, natural resources, and transportation connections, and wartime Defense Department spending had been extraordinarily good to Utah.

Olpin's first acts were to secure what was already in place, including contracts the University of Utah held with the U.S. Atomic Energy Commission (AEC) and U.S. Army Ordnance. Immediately after his arrival, he began making speeches about the awful responsibility of sustaining America's scientific leadership. He stated that he could see scientists taking over the responsibility not only for supporting but leading society. Applying war-learned lessons, he said, could produce huge advancements in a peacetime world. These he enumerated in three fundamental steps: 1) the use of atomic energy, "a double-edged weapon which may snuff out or fan to greater brilliance the flame of civilization"; 2) the development of the "project type" of research exemplified in the atomic-bomb experiment, where all sorts of knowledge are coordinated to achieve a set goal (in contrast to the old "idea type," where a lone thinker struck out on his own and his labor was often wasted); and 3) the freeing of man from the limits of the wheel, for example with jet propulsion. "In time this may mean growth of great inland civilizations, whereas all previous societies have clustered along waterways,"[25] he predicted to audiences whom he encouraged to take pride in their good geographical fortune.

Olpin painted visions of the future where travelers would be riding "air chariots, in extreme comfort, to any part of the globe, in 60 hours."[26] He said this to Rotarians. He told it to wool growers, copper miners, admen, and forgers of steel. In each of these industries, Olpin challenged leaders to adopt a new, international orientation; not to let mountain barriers force a "hemmed-in" way of thinking.

For his inauguration, Olpin invited experts from industry, science, and social science to join him in offering insights about the past and future of Utah. By the time the ceremony occurred on October 16, 1946, the focus of the symposium, "Utah: The Next Fifty Years," had shifted slightly. It featured a string of experts weighing in with their views of the University of Utah's role and contributions to the development of key industries in the state. Henry Eyring, the dean of the university's new graduate school and one of the nation's experts on theoretical and experimental atomic research, was featured on the podium. Olpin also paid homage to two of his mentors at Ohio State University who attended: James Lewis Morrill, who had organized the OSU Research Foundation and gone on to become president of the University of Minnesota, and his former boss, President Howard L. Bevis. Media coverage of the ceremonies underscored that never had the University of Utah received the kind of adulation that accompanied Olpin's inauguration. There were representatives wearing the colorful drapes and hoods of more than seventy-five of the nation's colleges and universities.

The accolades also seemed to ignite in Olpin a chain reaction of urgent educational tasks aimed at managing not just national, but global, problems in the wake of World War II. He described the pressure from society on state universities to help the U.S. make remarkable strides in producing "superior" men and women while simultaneously helping to create new jobs for them to fill. Heralding the coming of Utah's Geneva Steel, Governor Herbert B. Maw wondered aloud whether, at the close of the first century of Utah history, "a century of struggle and hardship," a new era was dawning. Olpin concluded the proceedings by emphasizing his resolve to keep the desert ever blooming, conducive to new and vigorous growth.[27]

Under Olpin's direction, others at the university began to adopt his anything-is-possible vision, a mixture of national idealism, naiveté, and brilliance. Staffing was a major focus. The president would gladly have done each job himself if his duties had permitted it, but Olpin started searching for the best possible person to manage the administration of governmental and private research contracts for the university. He knew that basic science was neither understood nor appreciated by the mass of humanity and that most scientific capital had come from overseas before the war. Olpin wrote to his old friend Clyde Williams of the Battelle Memorial Institute in Columbus, Ohio, asking permission to recruit the director of Battelle's research-education division, Robert Van Pelt.[28] When Van Pelt wouldn't come to Utah, Olpin fixed his sights on Elmo Morgan.

Among other things, Olpin needed someone to oversee the specifications of a radiation research laboratory being built under contract for the AEC. The plutonium and radon to be tested in it would require top-level clearance and materials control. Morgan, who had managed the development of federal programs, including the installations that produced the world's first atomic bomb, won the job and oversaw the work. He briefed Olpin every step of the way as they negotiated details such as the amount of compensation for teaching faculty conducting research for outside entities. It was often the federal government's view that states and students should bear most of that expense, and there was a great deal of give and take over appropriate research overhead costs. An aid in this kind of accounting was Olpin's four-quarter plan, which allowed payments to staff members by outside agencies for work performed in their nonteaching session.

In 1950–51, the total value of research grants and projects was $1,130,000. When Morgan arrived from Los Alamos in September 1951, the university employed forty-one principal investigators, who were conducting cooperative research for the U.S. military, U.S. Public Health Service, American Cancer Society, National Foundation for Infantile Paralysis, and Utah Department of Health in the Utah Engineering Experiment Station in the College of Mines and Mineral Industries, as well as the areas of chemistry, physics, mathematics, psychology anatomy, bacteriology, biochemistry, obstetrics and gynecology, pathology, pediatrics, pharmacy, physiology, psychiatry, public health, preventive medicine, radiology, and surgery.[29] In a memo to twenty-nine head researchers, Morgan explained the main responsibilities of his job. It said that he was to make sure that the contracting party and the research worker carried out their obligations and were satisfied.[30]

He did this so well that one top U.S. bureaucrat said that all universities' research programs could be administered more effectively if there were more Elmo Morgans. After the Booz, Allen, and Hamilton university-management report recommendations, Morgan was promoted to business vice president. In that capacity, he played a key role in successfully lobbying the 1957 state legislature to appropriate funds for planning and initial construction of classrooms, laboratories, and teaching and research facilities for a University of Utah Medical Center. Apparently other state leaders saw his value, too, because in 1958, Governor George Dewey Clyde asked Morgan to assume the directorship of the Utah State Department of Highways. From that bureaucratic position, Morgan went on to become business vice president of the statewide system of the University of California.

Meanwhile, Utah researchers carried out projects about the relationship between health and man-made environmental hazards. Most of the funds came from outside Utah, particularly from United States Department of Defense agencies; the Department of Health, Education and Welfare; the (AEC); the United States Department of Education; and the National Science Foundation. A grant from the U.S. Public Health Service funded a study to help determine the cancer hazards associated with the mining and milling of uranium ores and other radioactive materials. Addressing the topic of poor, sooty air in populated valleys, the State of Utah in 1953 appropriated $200,000 each to the University of Utah, the Utah Agricultural Experiment Station, and the Utah Department of Health for a coordinated study of the harmful effects of air pollution. Radiological and ecological studies were highly classified but were approved by the State Board of Regents between 1951 and 1953. During the 1953–54 fiscal year, a total of 118 projects were cooperatively funded at the University of Utah. Of them 69 were in the medical college and 49 in the remainder of the university.[31]

In early nuclear-medicine studies, researchers supported by the National Cancer Institute and the AEC studied the metabolism of elemental copper in subjects with and without liver disease.[32]

Under the direction of Carl Christensen, also funded by the AEC, the University of Utah conducted studies on the effects of atomic tests at Dugway Proving Ground. The army had established Dugway in 1942 for biological and chemical warfare testing. According to a report published by the Department of Energy's (DOE's) assistant secretary for environment, safety, and health in 1995, at least fourteen tests on the spread and containment of atomic releases were conducted at Dugway between 1949 and 1952. The report said, "Documentation uncovered in DOE's search…do[es] not show that human experimentation was involved in the Dugway tests. The only known evidence of human exposure reviewed involves a crane operator accidentally exposed during a tantalum test."[33]

Up to September 1962, the AEC had invested nearly $4 million in basic research of radiation-induced diseases in large animals on the university campus. To support this study, the university maintained one of the country's largest colonies of research dogs. With its contract to operate a radiation laboratory to study the effects of atomic bomb fallout, Morgan indicated that the university could conduct studies where animals were exposed to radiation either externally or by inhaling radioactive dust.[34] While the radiobiology studies supported by the AEC had diminished by 1953, the university's contract for work at Dugway for ecological study increased by $25,000; it included radiating food samples.[35] During that year, $219,680 was transferred to the university's general fund for overhead operations, approximately 40 percent for medical-school studies and 60 percent for projects in the rest of the university.[36]

The army asked Morgan to consult in weapons research and development, and so he visited the campuses of Ohio State, Maryland, Delaware, George Washington, Michigan State, Columbia, and Wisconsin Universities. Sounding very discouraged after his return, he reported to President Olpin, "The most impressive thing on each of these campuses was the large amount of new construction being done. Our effort is really 'peanuts' compared with what is going on on these other campuses. Any attraction which we might offer to entice faculty members or others to join us will have to come from something other than physical facilities. We are really in the dark ages."[37]

This concern echoes throughout the writing of Morgan's successor, Paul Hodson, who heralded the "mushrooming complexity of graduate and research program" and accompanying need for building as the *Crisis on Campus*.[38] As it

Explosives expert and research chemist Melvin A. Cook was in such demand that he gave up teaching and became a "dollar-a-year man" for the University of Utah.

did on so many U.S. university campuses, the Soviet Union's surpassing the United States in launching unmanned satellites to explore space had a redoubling effect on the University of Utah administration's push to expand laboratory space. The so-called Sputnik effect was a steady and driving force.

Research became the lifeblood of medical education. Intensive research into the nature and treatment of leukemia got under way at the University of Utah. During the late 1950s, researchers conducted studies on techniques for labeling white blood cells using phosphorous-32 with 120 inmates at the Utah State Prison. The studies were supported by the AEC and the U.S. Public Health Service. Investigators did not find toxic side effects or damage to white cells—validating the scientific approach used by Dr. Maxwell M. Wintrobe.[39]

Research by College of Medicine faculty members also led toward the development of the Salk polio vaccine. The college became recognized as a leading center for research on muscular dystrophy, which was proportionately more prevalent in Utah than most other parts of the United States. The number-two killer of Americans, cancer, was the focus of considerable basic research, as were the causes of high blood pressure and diabetes. Faculty members of the Department of Pharmacology undertook research into the cause and treatment of convulsive disorders. The total amount of annual support for College of Medicine research activities was approximately $3 million in 1962.[40]

Research on explosives was among the most prominent and lucrative new ventures for the University of Utah during this period, and metallurgist Melvin A. Cook was the lynchpin. The Institute of Metals and Explosives Research began as the Explosives Research Group to handle contracts with the armed services. In 1958 its name was changed, but it remained, more or less, the private research organization of its director, who held a professorship in metallurgy and contracts totaling $2,064,365 with the air force, the army, the navy, and the AEC.[41] Cook's lab trained thirty-four graduate students who earned Ph.D.s. They included personnel from the Sandia Corporation, the Iron Ore Company of Canada, Boeing

Aircraft, Kennecott Copper, Rio Tinto Zinc in Australia, and even the head of the University of Utah's Department of Ceramics. On March 29, 1960, Cook received a patent for a new, inexpensive slurry explosive that became the blasting agent of choice in most mining and construction projects.

Professor Cook then became president of Intermountain Research and Engineering Company (IRECO) in Salt Lake City and Mesabi Blasting Agents, Inc., in Minnesota, both of which became major suppliers of the new slurry explosives.[42] His private-sector workload and consulting agreements, including one with the University of California's Lawrence Livermore Laboratory, required that Cook give up teaching, but he technically remained a member of the faculty, receiving a dollar a year from the university to continue his affiliation as director of the Institute of Metals and Explosives Research.[43] Such an entrepreneurial arrangement, supported by Olpin, maintained Cook's academic standing, permitted the university to be credited in his numerous articles in national journals, and financed extensive fundamental research and student training.[44] Though Cook wasn't the only "dollar-a-year man" at the university during the Olpin era—in 1960 there were 345 faculty members with that status—he exemplified the new types of academic accommodation that were made to access the financial fuel that ran the engines of higher education.[45]

Also in the College of Mines was the Kennecott Research Center, which began operation in 1955. In the 1945–46 school year, Kennecott Copper Corporation made a $200,000 gift for research and study in the field of metal mining. Soon thereafter company officials expressed their interest in building a research laboratory near the university. The university offered Kennecott a forty-year lease on a building site on the northwest corner of 1st South and 15th East Streets with the proviso that at the end of the lease period, any buildings on the property would revert to the university. By early 1953, agreement was reached for a building estimated to cost the corporation $1.3 million, and the Kennecott Research Center began.[46]

Another addition to the university's research effort, construction of an atomic "teaching" reactor housed in the Merrill Engineering Building, was approved on March 10, 1952. University officials negotiated with the AEC's Idaho operations office in Arco over the purchase of a decommissioned, surplus reactor nicknamed "Susie." Reasons for housing a nuclear-research facility on campus included the significance of uranium mining in the Intermountain West and the number of people on the university staff experienced in atomic energy and radioactivity. It was the responsibility of the AEC's licensing and regulation division to control the

Inventor Melvin A. Cook demonstrated industrial uses of explosives research from the university's Institute of Metals and Explosives Research in Switzerland.

special nuclear material that furnished the neutron source for experiments in the nonmilitary use of uranium.[47]

A University Research Committee urged faculty members to initiate other, new projects and took special interest in assisting those areas of the school "which find it difficult or impossible to obtain research funds from outside sources."[48] The bulk of these small grants were for projects in the social sciences. In 1950 the University Research Committee set up a revolving fund of twenty thousand dollars to aid the University Press's publication program. Olpin felt that a first-rate research university must have a scholarly press.

Even his old nemesis J. Bracken Lee found Olpin and the university's research accomplishments remarkable: in 1955 he appointed Olpin to the Utah Committee on Industrial and Employment Planning. By the time that Olpin retired, expenditures for organized research projects had reached an estimated total of $7.5 million, an almost ninetyfold increase over the previous twenty years. On the average, two grants or contracts were being processed through the office of Cooperative Research per day. More than three hundred principal investigators were active on

The Kennecott Research Center was the hallmark of university/industry collaborative research. The copper company spent $1.3 million on this campus building in 1953.

The Tooele Ordnance Depot was the site of explosives and other cooperative research conducted by university faculty during the Olpin era.

these projects, and many other professional and nonprofessional personnel and students were actively engaged in research through training programs, fellowships, and graduate traineeships. Research groups, including the Radiobiology Laboratory, Metabologic Laboratory, and Henry Eyring and Carl Christensen's Institute for the Study of Rate Processes, had gained international fame.

Yet none had existed the year that Olpin had arrived and made application to fund an ore-dressing lab. In 1945 only $83,563 was available for all organized research at the University of Utah. As a consequence of these new funds for research, the university rapidly became one of the more important graduate schools in the United States. The *New York Times*, in a survey conducted in November 1959, ranked the University of Utah forty-eighth in the production of Ph.D. scholars in the United States. In 1961 the university became one of only thirty-one American colleges and universities subsidized to operate an Honors Program under the Ford Foundation Fund for the Advancement of Learning. The program was organized to enrich and improve the education of capable students, both undergraduates and master's degree candidates, and prepare them more rapidly for further graduate studies and college teaching.

CHAPTER 5

SPREADING WORLDLY AMBITION

With the university's expansion to accommodate veterans came a growing sense that education was integral to the United States, including its international position and national defense. The atomic bomb, the cold war, and Sputnik had especially profound effects upon university leaders, who were expected to unite science and industry to maintain America's moral and economic competitive edge. These concepts held special appeal for Olpin, who was an ardent internationalist and a wise opportunist. He felt closely related to the allies who had fought and won World War II, but because he had served a mission for the Church of Jesus Christ of Latter-day Saints in Japan, he was deeply influenced by Asian culture. "All my life I have been interested in person-to-person relationships with peoples of foreign lands," he told members of the Fulbright scholars council, and his actions proved it.[1]

Olpin interrupted his studies at Brigham Young University to perform a four-year volunteer mission, returning to Utah in 1920. Citing his preference for sleeping on a futon on the floor, not once during his years as a missionary did he spend a night in a Western-style hotel. One university publicist claimed Olpin's time in Japan forged in his mind "sympathetic vibrations" between two of the world's most beautiful peaks: sacred Fujiyama, inland from Tokyo, and Provo's Mount Timpanogos, in whose shadow A. Ray and Elva Olpin had both been raised. "Japan's holy mountain symbolized to him the need for his own hill-rimmed university to reach not only just beyond its compact valley but also into distant corners of a fast-shrinking world," wrote *Utah Alumnus* editor Paul Cracroft.[2] Olpin's facility with Japanese and the diplomatic edge he felt this gave him were an immense source of pride. Throughout his life, he stayed close to Japan.

At Bell Telephone Laboratories, Olpin translated patents into Japanese. If he got stuck on a word, he used it as an excuse to wend his way through New York's Greenwich Village to find a Japanese student attending New York University. He knew several graduate students there, living in garrets heated only by potbellied stoves, and he gladly climbed the stairs to their attic apartments just to converse in Japanese. Olpin also felt that his early career at Bell Labs had enabled him to play a part in changing the way that nearly everyone on earth lived: he had helped structure the photoelectric element into the photocell and camera tube of television. In 1927 he had been part of the first team to demonstrate the practicality of TV and helped design and construct part of the equipment used in its famous first test.

Olpin visited Japan often and kept in touch with friends and dignitaries in his former host country, turning these early relationships into international educational opportunities during and even after his presidency. In 1963 he offered to host ten students selected by the Nagoya Broadcasting Corporation to come to Utah on an educational tour. Associate Vice President for Academic Affairs Boyer Jarvis worked with the U.S. Information Service's American Cultural Center in the Department of Foreign Service to coordinate arrangements for what became an annual visit by students from Nagoya. The University of Utah provided a three-week orientation that included seminars on the philosophical and historical origins of American society, characteristics of twentieth-century American life and culture, the cultural geography of the United States, and American sociological problems along with various aspects of American business, science, and technology.[3] The first of these Nagoya Broadcasting Corporation study tours to Utah commemorated the tenth anniversary of the Nagoya television station, but the visits continued annually for twenty years.

After Olpin retired in 1964, he remained at the university and was reassigned to develop intercultural programs. His old friend J. L. Morrill from Ohio State University was then a program consultant for Latin American development at the Ford Foundation. Olpin wrote to him soliciting work in intercultural affairs, but nothing materialized. Under the direction of the Asia Foundation in 1965, he spent six months advising the president of Korea's Seoul National University in building the school's international stature.

Together with the mayor of Matsumoto, Olpin established a sister-city relationship between that city on central Honshu Island, in Nagano Prefecture, and

Utah's capital city. This was part of the Eisenhower administration's "People to People" program, but it was also emblematic of Olpin's belief that knowledge of world culture only comes through the exchange of personnel, whether they are students, faculty, businessmen, top officials of government, or ordinary citizens.[4]

For a small-town boy, Olpin had a powerful sense of connection to the world. This was manifested in the university's establishment of an Institute of World Affairs, the model United Nations assembly for high school seniors, and a world tour that he undertook in 1959 to organize university study abroad. He wanted international, intercultural awareness to run throughout the whole educational process—not just be limited to isolated courses on international relations. Technical and professional training of personnel who could serve federal agencies in international administration became a focused goal of Olpin's administration. He tapped political scientist and historian G. Homer Durham for his talent in organizing these institutes and centers.[5]

The founding of an Institute of Government under his direction in 1946 and the establishment of an Institute of World Affairs the same year permitted the coordination and organization of courses dealing with international affairs. Directed by the dean of the Graduate School of Social Work and chairman of the Department of Sociology, Arthur Beeley, the Institute of World Affairs held periodic conferences, conducted quarterly seminars, promoted exchanges of foreign students, collected and published scholarly material, and fostered the organization of study groups at the university and throughout the state.[6]

The Institute of World Affairs was succeeded in 1956 by the Institute of International Studies under the direction of S. Grover "Sam" Rich Jr. of the political-science department, who had been U.S. Department of State vice consul to Spain from 1942 to 1946.[7] An advocate for national-security studies on American campuses, Rich orchestrated a certificate in international relations that emphasized American military strategy and tactics and their relationship to U.S. foreign policy. Graduates of the program went on to work as U.S. foreign-service officers with the Department of State, the Department of Defense, the U.S. Information Agency, the Central Intelligence Agency, and the Agency for International Development (AID).[8]

Also in 1956, the university created an Institute of American Studies, which had an international component because it emphasized knowledge of the roots of American culture in other civilizations. The institute was under the direction of a professor of American literature, William Mulder. In 1959 a new Center for Language and Intercultural Studies was created. It was a coordinating office designed to work with and through established departments to promote interdisciplinary studies, particularly of the cultures and civilizations of the Middle East, Asia, and Africa. This focus on the East, founding director Mulder explained, was designed to balance out most students' exclusive orientation to the West, an orientation that "permeates our whole heritage and in our curriculum pretty well takes care of itself."[9]

Not long after the center's conception, the "language" aspect was dropped from its title, and the word "International" was substituted for "Intercultural." So renamed, the Institute of International Studies functioned as liaison for students interested in positions with the foreign service, the Department of State, the U.S. Information Agency, the Department of Defense, and similar agencies.[10] With University of Utah Dean Sterling McMurrin's encouragement, its second director, Professor Mulder, went off to teach

English professor William Mulder was the director of the University of Utah's Center for Language and Intercultural Studies, later called the Institute of International Studies. He taught in India twice during the Olpin years.

Milton and Melville at the University of Delhi in India as a Fulbright fellow in 1957–58 to enhance his own international perspective.[11] "This appointment comes as an honor both to Professor Mulder and the University and is obviously very much in the interest of our political, economic, and cultural relations with India," wrote McMurrin to G. Homer Durham.[12] The U.S. government had established the Fulbright program in 1946 to provide international exchanges of scholars.

The federal government and private foundations helped to fuel the university's growing involvement with world affairs. Both sought the participation and counsel of academics in formulating a response to America's space race with the Soviet Union. It is important to note that the university's international-affairs programs were organized in the context of major federal initiatives such as the National Defense Education Act (NDEA) to advance study in science, math, and modern foreign languages. Mulder explained how much Olpin wanted to secure federal support for the university's international program:

> When the NDEA came along we saw that as an opportunity to get funding for language and area studies. We were overly ambitious. We submitted plans for every area—Latin America, Asia, Middle East, Africa. With Hal Bentley, Olpin and I went East to the

officers of the NDEA and talked to them in great detail about how to prepare an application....

The whole idea behind NDEA was national defense because the politicians knew that only for defense purposes could we get money. That was the way to make our country more sophisticated than it had been. And one of President Olpin's achievements was to convince back east officials that as the result of missionary activity we had a big resource in languages and we could draw upon that.[13]

The development of foreign-studies programs at other U.S. universities was also subsidized by the Ford and Rockefeller Foundations, which encouraged adding expertise on a foreign area or culture to proficiency in a discipline, such as political science or economics. "Not all of us will receive the large quantities of money from the foundations which will permit the specialized area study such as is being followed at the Russian Institute at Columbia, Harvard, and the Yale Institute. However, I feel that it is important that most, if not all our state universities, attempt, even in a limited and modest way, to contribute something to the training of personnel for the important needs of international administration," Olpin told colleagues at a meeting of the National Association of State Universities in 1951.[14] So-called area studies at the University of Utah certified students as geographically and culturally adept in understanding issues facing Latin America, Asia, or the Middle East. The concentration on the Middle East, begun at the University of Utah in 1959 and supported by a thirty-seven-thousand-dollar matching grant from the NDEA, rapidly produced doctoral candidates in economics, education, sociology, languages, zoology, and political science.

Olpin's interest in relating the university to the world made a great leap forward when he persuaded Egyptian scholar Aziz S. Atiya to join the faculty as a professor of language and history. Atiya had impeccable, truly world-class credentials. The two met by chance in Cairo when Olpin visited that city, where Atiya lived. In the fall of 1959, the president went abroad to investigate opportunities to exchange faculty and students with foreign universities in sixteen countries, particularly Japan and India. He also visited a Ford Foundation project of the university's to help improve the teaching of business administration in Burma. Olpin happened to fly into Egypt on the same airplane as Professor Arnold S. Nash, who taught religion at the University of North Carolina in Chapel Hill. Nash was a houseguest of Aziz Atiya and his wife, Lola. Olpin's driver failed to turn up at the airport in Egypt, but the Atiyas recognized the man from Utah. Atiya had been a guest lecturer at the University of Utah two years before, and afterward Olpin and the Board of Regents had invited him to join them for lunch in the old Union Building.

Egyptian scholar and professor Aziz S. Atiya played a key role in the university's international affairs.

Atiya's 1951 American lecture tour had included Princeton, Yale, Johns Hopkins, Stanford, and Utah Universities and the University of Michigan. He later recalled that nowhere in the world had he been treated more hospitably than in Salt Lake City. "The Atiyas insisted on entertaining me to repay what they said was the best reception they had in the U.S.," Olpin wrote in his travel diary. The Atiyas toured the Coptic Museum in Cairo with Olpin, took him on a camel ride to the pyramids, hosted him in their home for dinner, and showed him "the best private library of Egyptian materials extant"[15] —*their* library.

Atiya held a foundation chair in medieval history at the University of Alexandria, Egypt, where he became the first president of Coptic studies. He was also the first Fulbright exchange professor to the United States from Egypt. Yet he was restless to make a lasting legacy somewhere.

Atiya had been sent at the age of five from his small village to a school in Cairo. When he was twenty-nine, he received a diploma from the Higher Training College and moved on to the University of Liverpool in England, where he was a fellow and tutor in the School of Oriental Studies. In 1931 he earned a bachelor's degree in medieval and modern history with first-class honors. He transferred to the University of London and completed his doctorate in Arabic and Islamic studies. By the time of the publication of his thesis on the Crusade of Nicropolis, Atiya could speak thirteen languages. In 1950 he received a Fulbright travel award to study ancient manuscripts from the Monastery of St. Catherine at Mount Sinai at the Library of Congress in Washington, D.C.

An authority recognized by the American Medieval Academy, he was highly sought after by universities worldwide, but his wife and children were enchanted by Utah. The Atiyas were members of the Coptic faith, which according to Olpin "claimed to perpetuate the early Christian principles and practices,"[16] proclaiming Egypt as the only land in the world to be honored and blessed by a visit from the Holy Family. Yet, among the Mormon faithful, the Atiyas somehow felt at home in Utah's Zion. Knowing that Atiya longed to share his appreciation for Egyptian culture outside his native country, Olpin made several offers to him over the years to return to Utah on a permanent basis.

When Lola Atiya confided to her husband that Salt Lake City was the only place she could imagine raising their two children and living out their lives following retirement, Atiya finally accepted Olpin's offer to become a professor of languages and history at the University of Utah. In Salt Lake City, Atiya's religious studies were taken as serious, academic activities. His primary duties were teaching and building a Middle East library; administrators felt that to capitalize on Atiya's talents, they must not saddle him too heavily with administrative responsibilities. Besides, as Department of Political Science Chair Roy V. Peel observed, the authorities in Washington supplying funds would prefer or even require that the director of the Middle East program be an American citizen.[17]

Federal officials with the NDEA issued two more consecutive grants to the University of Utah. These enabled Atiya to return to the Middle East to purchase and arrange donations to the George Thomas Library's Middle East collection. These included, for instance, one of three known sets of the chanted Koran. The set consists of seventy-six long-playing recordings of the Moslem scriptures in North African dialects.

Olpin was extremely proud of Atiya's scholarly pursuits, contacts, and worldly experiences, which he believed qualified Atiya—and by extension the university— to interpret world problems, particularly those relating to the Near East and the West. In 1960 Atiya gave Olpin notice that he planned, over seven years, to donate to the university's library his private collection of 109 ancient papyri and 108 paper and parchment archival documents, which ranged from the ninth to the nineteenth century AD. In 1962 he became director of the Middle East Center.

The Atiyas eventually donated to the university hundreds of thousands of dollars worth of rare books, magazines, ancient Arabic papyri, and antiquities from

Aboard the USS Iowa, Olpin learned of the 1953 Korean War armistice. He thought it heightened the importance of his upcoming Department of State mission against Communism.

their personal collection of Arabic texts. The collection distinguished the University of Utah as having one of the three best Middle East libraries in the United States, Atiya said in 1963. The twelve-thousand-volume library was then located in the university's former bookstore. "My only hope is that the great structure that I had envisioned from the beginning will grow again into an institution of everlasting value for the humanities and for America," Atiya told historian Everett Cooley.[18]

One of Olpin's final acts as president was to oversee naming the Aziz S. Atiya Library for Middle East studies. He knew and told others that finding Atiya had been one of the most important accomplishments of his lifetime.[19] This was an especially significant acknowledgement, considering the foresight that Olpin showed in harvesting from many different resources the money and talent that he devoted to intercultural scholarship.

The most profound of Olpin's international sojourns as president led him to formulate a plan that he felt led seven years later to the creation of the U.S. Peace Corps. Following World War II, the Department of State solicited input from higher-education leaders about improving the United States' foreign image and staving off Communism. Olpin received a three-month commission from the leaders and specialists branch's Educational Exchange Division to survey educational conditions in Japan and New Zealand. Surely he must have been selected for the assignment because of his proficiency with the Japanese language. From August

President Olpin wrote his plan for an international youth service after this 1953 assignment to Australia, New Zealand, and Japan for the U.S. Department of State. He thought the Olpin Plan led to the creation of the Peace Corps.

through October 1953, Olpin inspected universities and private and public research labs in practically every major city in both countries.

What the Department of State received after Olpin's return were pointed suggestions for radically reforming American diplomacy. Olpin began preaching a new role for American higher education in improving mutual understanding by preparing students for foreign-service assignments. "I returned from Japan and a trip around the world more firmly convinced than ever that the leadership of America in the world can best be maintained by a restoration of the missionary system," he reported.[20] That experience led him to suggest that universities train "ambassadors of the American way" to engage in service abroad. He went so far in his recommendations to the Department of State to detail, point by point, the advantages of training and placing students in voluntary foreign-service roles, following the missionary system perfected by the Church of Jesus Christ of Latter-day Saints.

Olpin became so persistent in circulating what he called "The Olpin Plan for Mutual Understanding and Trust between the Peoples of the World and the People of the United States" around Washington that, when Senator and presidential hopeful John F. Kennedy challenged America's young to serve the country in the cause of peace, Olpin felt that his great idea was finally being put into action. He also felt quite certain that the U.S. Peace Corps was a plagiarism of what he and his administrators referred to on a daily basis as "the Olpin Plan."[21] Philosopher and Dean of the College of Arts and Sciences Sterling McMurrin carried the missionary zeal of the Olpin Plan with him on a U.S. Department of State special assignment to keep Communism in check at the University of Tehran. After witnessing the Iranians' susceptibility to the Russian message, he wrote, "I am more converted than ever to the importance of the principles and techniques envisioned by the Olpin plan."[22] Numerous copies of the plan were left in Olpin's presidential papers, and he often cited it in articles and speeches.

His little-known legacy to the Peace Corps became a drumbeat throughout the rest of his career. Nearly a decade before Kennedy's admonition for citizens "to ask what you can do for your country," A. Ray Olpin was lobbying for similar action as a way of improving America's postwar foreign relations: "preaching Americanism by precept and example."[23] Inept foreign-service officials and embarrassing behavior by American troops consorting with Japanese women during the occupation, he felt, posed a dual threat to America's image. Anti-Americanism was a greater threat than Communism to the dominant leadership of the United States worldwide, he said.[24] He called for greater respect for the social barriers that proscribed intimate relations between East Asian women, whom he called Orientals, and American men, or Occidentals.[25] The real tragedy resulting from the presence of our armies in Japan, he continued, comes from the fact that thousands of half-caste children are being born out of wedlock. Attractive though these youngsters may be, they have no social standing in either Japan or America.[26]

The solution to damaging actions by careless U.S. representatives, he proposed, was engaging U.S. higher education to teach cultural awareness and offer technical training for ambassadors of the American way to be placed in voluntary, foreign-community service—particularly in Hiroshima, Japan, "that devastated city, stricken by the first atomic bomb."[27]

The university's president went to great lengths to get the Olpin Plan into the hands of Washington's decision makers. In 1959 he became especially determined to see the plan put into operation. He pursued the U.S. Department of Education for a contract to start one of the country's first campus-based training centers. Armed with a further elaboration of his 1953 plan, he attended a meeting of the Institute for International Education where participants discussed the idea of foreign service with Senators Hubert Humphrey and J. William Fulbright.[28] Edward R. Murrow chaired the meeting, and Dean Rusk, who became secretary of state and was serving then as president of the Rockefeller Foundation, offered Olpin a sympathetic ear. However, his insistence on modeling international service after Christian missions was a bureaucratic stumbling block that Olpin was unable to surmount. He staked his position in the matter against Senator Fulbright, who held a key policy position as chair of the U.S. Senate Committee on Foreign Relations. Congress had named the Fulbright program that fostered mutual understanding among nations through educational and cultural exchanges for him. Senator Fulbright wrote Olpin that "the one point that bothered me most in your plan for creating greater understanding and trust between the people of the world and the people of the United States is your use of the word missionary."[29]

Olpin was less pragmatic. He refused to concede the conceptual link between missionary work and education-for-service and eventually switched from pursing federal financing to seeking private foundation support for his plan. He confided to Utah Senator Wallace F. Bennett that a private sponsor such as Nelson Rockefeller might be a preferable source of funding. "Certainly, we would have more freedom of operation and less need to confirm with State Department or Civil Service regulations," he observed.[30] Bennett agreed that this tactic would put Olpin's plan for a cultural missionary program on safer ground.[31]

However, this did not prove to be a successful strategy for selling the Olpin Plan, either. Utahns had been recognized for their penchant for international education since World War I. American philanthropist Andrew Carnegie's endowment established the Institute of International Education (IIE) in New York City and charged it to engage U.S. higher education in sustaining America's international leadership. Internationalist and New York political scientist Stephen Duggan was the IIE's founding director. Olpin had read Duggan's biography, *A Professor at Large,* where the author stated,

> I then determined to visit the chief universities and colleges of our own country to acquaint them with my plans in order, if possible, to secure their cooperation. I found practically all enthusiastic about the idea and eager to assist in its realization, for all knew the ignorance of our people in international affairs. To my amazement, the institution where I found students best informed on foreign affairs was on neither the Atlantic nor the Pacific seaboard but in the far interior, at the University of Utah. At that time, 1919, the University though non-sectarian was still controlled by the Mormons, and it was customary for the Mormon students before graduating to spend a year abroad as missionaries.[32]

Despite the university's credentials in international education, it did not, during Olpin's lifetime, receive the recognition or the financial support for international service that he felt was due it. Harold Bentley, dean of the Extension Division, wound up rewriting the Olpin Plan and submitting it with a draft bill to authorize a youth-service corps to the fledgling Kennedy administration. Bentley's version of the legislation authorizing a United States service corps requested a $50 million appropriation. It would also authorize the corps to enlist educational institutions to grant "academic and/or teaching credit for members of the Corps."[33]

Bentley's initiative came as a shock to Olpin,[34] but after securing the president's blessing, Bentley carried what had originally been the Olpin Plan to a meeting with the Kennedy team ultimately credited with implementing the Peace Corps as an agency in 1961.[35] In his cover letter, Bentley predicted that once the president-elect put his imprint on it, this voluntary-service program would become known the world over as "the Kennedy Plan." Congress commissioned nearby Colorado State University to put the plan into action.

The Olpin Plan became just a footnote in the designs of other educationists who consulted Kennedy and his brother-in-law, R. Sargent Shriver, who was appointed to lead the Peace Corps. Yet Olpin's 1953 report to the U.S. Department of State proposing "civilian missions abroad" was included with descriptions of Peace Corps–type proposals among John F. Kennedy's presidential records.[36]

On March 22, 1961, Utah Congressman David S. King arranged to introduce Olpin to the Peace Corps' new director in Washington. Hoping that the University of Utah would become a favored site for the training of Peace Corps volunteers, Olpin handed Shriver a fresh copy of the Olpin Plan. "All my life," he said, "I have been interested in person-to-person relationships with peoples of foreign lands." According to Olpin, Morris Abrams, general counsel for the Peace Corps, then remarked that "he had read the recommendations that I had written in 1953 and he was amazed at the similarity between what I had suggested and what was being done at the present time, even though there was eight years elapsed between the time I had recommended the Olpin Plan and they had established the Peace Corps."[37]

A month later, Olpin told the Board of Regents that Shriver had invited the University of Utah to submit proposals for directing missions to countries that would receive Peace Corps aid.[38] While other universities were commissioned, the University of Utah was not awarded a full-fledged Peace Corps training contract until 1963–64.[39]

A more public setback for the Olpin administration's international activities took place in a slow diplomatic drama played out in Addis Ababa, Ethiopia—the hub of the United States' foreign-aid activities in East Africa. The university secured a contract with the U.S. AID's International Cooperation Administration (ICA) to survey the needs of higher education in Ethiopia. In the fall of 1959, Olpin met the U.S. ambassador to Ethiopia in northeastern Africa to pave the way for the arrival of a team of seven specialists from the University of Utah. Bentley was named chairman of the survey team and given a three-months' leave of absence from November 30, 1959 until February 29, 1960. Collaborating in Ethiopia with Bentley were Grant Calder, head of the university's community development and business services; Dr. Philip Price, dean of the College of Medicine; Willard Blaesser, dean of students; William Burke from chemistry, Grant Borg from civil engineering, and Paul Fawley from educational administration.

On Christmas Eve 1959, the third day after the team's arrival, Price recorded in his journal that conferences with key officials had given the Utah team a sense of the complexity of problems facing the unique country. Their own political missteps would make a delicate situation even more fragile. Members of Congress threatened to cut appropriations to universities involved in foreign educational operations through the ICA. While Olpin defended the ICA's university-contract programs as a form of foreign aid that strengthened the United States' position against Russia, the Utah consultants found themselves delivering detailed strategy to no one in particular.[40]

Olpin claimed he was personally involved in making arrangements with the U.S. embassy for the Utah consultants to be presented to Ethiopian Emperor Haile

Selassie I or "HIM," as the American visitors called His Imperial Majesty among themselves. In a monarchy, protocol is essential, and gaining an audience with Selassie was an on-again, off-again endeavor that took six weeks to consummate. Speaking for the group, Bentley expressed the team's desire to assist in the imperial Ethiopian government's planning and building an educational institution based on the solid foundation stones of autonomy, academic freedom, ample resources, and official support. Bascom Story, chief education advisor to the Ethiopian-United States Cooperative Education Program, praised the survey team's performance in a letter to Olpin. "Our modern world hasn't as many frontiers as the world of our fathers and grandfathers—unless they be in Africa. So we have found this assignment a privilege and challenge as well as an interesting task," wrote Price in his journal's fourth and final installment.[41]

But the glow of romanticism expressed in week ten of the African consultancy dimmed considerably when the team's recommendations weren't implemented and a different group of American advisors was sent in to finish the job. In the end, it became clear that the primary client for the report was Selassie, not the U.S. government. The emperor pledged his full support and even gave his ancestral palace and grounds to become the hub of a campus for the university, which was to be substantially financed by the United States' ICA. At an impressive and colorful ceremony, Haile Selassie I University was founded on December 18, 1961. Olpin attended as guest of the imperial court, representing the National Association of State Universities, as well as the University of Utah. Bentley took a second leave of absence—this time for a full year—from the University of Utah to serve as acting president and academic vice president of the new Ethiopian university. He returned to Addis Ababa in the fall of 1961 to organize the administration of the new school. The ICA aided him by offering the University of Utah a contract to start a College of Education at the new Haile Selassie I University.

After being named acting president of the Ethiopian university, Bentley was befriended by a sociologist from Chicago, Donald Levine. Levine had also been an educational consultant in Ethiopia and had published a critical article, "Hailie Selassie's Ethiopia—Myth or Reality?" Citing a failed coup of Ethiopia's leadership by the imperial bodyguard, Levine questioned Selassie's commitment to democratic educational principles. Against Olpin's and the Department of State's recommendations, Bentley hired Levine to join him in Ethiopia as a consultant. Shortly thereafter recommendations by Bentley to fund staff, operations, and capital improvements were thwarted by the Ethiopian university's Board of Governors. Selassie controlled the board because he was minister of education and chancellor

Olpin congratulates Ethiopian dictator Haile Selassie for turning his palace into a university, with help from University of Utah educational advisors.

of the university, even though the nation's minister of finance was its titular chair. Bentley told Selassie that hiring Levine would be an impressive sign of his commitment to academic freedom. The emperor, as head of state, then said he could not guarantee the safety of Levine or his family and refused to approve his visa. Bentley had to stop Levine, who had by then arrived in Rome en route to Addis Ababa. This humiliated Bentley.

Other defying actions by the board, which appeared to be penalizing Bentley, included canceling meetings where he was scheduled to be present and holding meetings without him. Peace Corps officials viewed Bentley's accepting a post in the AID-financed Ethiopian university while working for the ICA as a conflict of interest and violation of its regulations.[42] Bentley began to sense his impotence, as his letter to President Olpin on May 3, 1962, suggested:

<blockquote>You will understand I am sure that I came here to help establish the kind of institution that our survey team has recommended. If it seems possible to go on with this kind of institution, certainly we would feel obligated to attempt to do so. If there is going to continue to be a great deal of political maneuvering and hassling without the kind of support that is required to resolve problems that result from opposing political and personal interests, I would see no point in remaining or dragging out the experience to a final dull ending.[43]</blockquote>

Bentley also sent a memorandum to the emperor where he requested to resign as acting president to devote himself full time to his alternate position as academic vice president. The emperor's private secretary responded by mail two weeks later. The reply said that His Imperial Majesty accepted Bentley's resignation, thanked him for his continual efforts, and added that a president would be appointed in the near future. Bentley had hoped that Bascom Story, also a member of the African university's Board of Governors and head of U.S. Peace Corps operations in Ethiopia, would be appointed president. Instead, Selassie appointed as new president Kassa Wolde Mariam, his granddaughter's husband and an Ethiopian.

Bentley wrote to the university's new president, asking that Levine be compensated for his past consulting work and his aborted trip and seeking permission to return to the United States to meet with Levine. President Kassa promptly terminated Levine's contract. Levine wrote to Bentley, criticizing his actions and predicting that the new president would pick Bentley's brains and then force him out. Within two weeks, Harold Bentley and his wife were quietly leaving Addis Ababa on a flight to New York City. President Kassa had given him vague instructions and ten days' per-diem expense reimbursement to recruit faculty from the United States. Bentley seemed tacitly to know that he would not return. Kassa terminated Bentley's contract, and he was without a job, either in Ethiopia or Salt Lake City.

Even worse, the university lost out on a Peace Corps contract to train two hundred teacher volunteers, sixty-four nurses and technicians, twenty educational-television specialists, and fifty adult-education and extension specialists to work in Ethiopia. The University of Utah still held a $680,000 contract with the AID to provide faculty for the College of Education at the Haile Selassie I University, and Olpin thought the university's Ethiopian experiences would give Utah a leg up when Ethiopia became one of the first countries to accept American Peace Corps volunteers. Olpin viewed selection to create a Peace Corps training center at the University of Utah as important recognition of the role it had already played in providing technical assistance and foreign aid to the country. Instead, the Peace Corps training contract went to a consortium of universities in the Washington, D.C., area, including Georgetown, George Washington, Howard, and the University of

Maryland. The University of Utah was invited to contract with the Peace Corps to develop a radio and educational-television station at Haile Selassie I University. Before Olpin could frame a response, he received a letter from President Kassa asking the University of Utah to provide twelve scholarships for Ethiopians to study education in Utah. Olpin politely declined.

In 1963 Olpin spent three months in Japan studying visual aids to facilitate teaching and expedite learning, including closed-circuit and open-circuit television, radio, and other electronic and mechanical equipment. He conducted his research in Japanese. This was ten years after he had gone to Japan under the Leaders and Specialists Exchange program of the U.S. Department of State, and he found the spread of television throughout the mountainous country and its potential for educational broadcasting "miraculous."[44] The study was funded by a grant from the Ford Foundation, administered by the IIE.

But to Olpin, being selected to form a Peace Corps training center was essential to a university's international credibility. He saw person-to-person foreign service as vital to breaking down the ivory-tower mentality that he felt separated universities from communities and Americans from the undeveloped world. But the university did not receive its first contract for training Peace Corps volunteers for Ethiopia until 1965—after Olpin had retired. The District of Columbia academic consortium was awarded the first two training-program contracts for Ethiopia, and UCLA won the next year's contracts for teacher training. While still in Ethiopia, Bentley had warned Olpin that it looked as though Kennedy special presidential assistant Harris Wofford wanted Washington-area institutions to get first crack at Africa. "Naturally we have been disappointed in the way the Peace Corps maneuvering has been conducted," Bentley confided.[45] Still, the University of Utah was instrumental in bringing technical and administrative aid from Salt Lake City to Ethiopia as it founded the first university in its three-thousand-year history.

Olpin described the cause of the university's successes and disappointing setbacks in forging links to the wider world as a duality he called "cosmopolitan provincialism." Founders of the University of Utah, possibly the oldest state university west of the Missouri, prided themselves in establishing an institution that matched the interests and educational needs of the surrounding community. That community was shaped by the LDS population, whose worldwide membership and missionary work naturally elicited interest in foreign countries and peoples. These characteristics, however, made the people both cosmopolitan and provincial, he explained in one of the most heartfelt speeches of his career. His 1955 speech to the Newcomen Society in North America, "Cosmopolitan Provincialism Utah!," was a reflection on the university's pioneer heritage and Olpin's present-day concerns about Utah's place in the world of learning. In it he observed that the cosmopolitanism of the University of Deseret, the University of Utah's parent school, stemmed from the church to which the pioneers claimed allegiance and the proselyting activities of its leaders."[46]

Mormon missionaries' acquaintance with the cultures of many countries and their proficiency in many languages constituted an excellent opportunity to exchange ideas on an international scale, the president proclaimed. Yet the tight social order of the Latter-day Saints, their experiments in communal living, their code of personal behavior demanding abstinence from tea, coffee, tobacco, and liquor, and their persistent reference to all others—Christians, Jews, and pagans alike—as "gentiles" "led to frequent misunderstanding on the part of those not of their faith. By these evidences it is obvious that the colonizers of Utah were decidedly provincial, but it can be shown that at the same time they were cosmopolitan, for their religion…exhorted them to seek knowledge, if not understanding, of other cultures."[47]

In the speech, Olpin then traced the effects of this cosmopolitan provincialism on the industrial and institutional development of the state. Though he did not lay claim to the sentiments, he quoted an 1856 sermon by Orson Pratt, mathematician, classical scholar, and an outstanding astronomer for his time. Pratt was impatient for improvements to the University of Deseret. He said, "We have had a university in name, but we have had no such university," Olpin continued, "The vision of the early settlers seemed to be diminishing.… Instructors were branded with near heresy if they encouraged diversity in the thinking of their students. There was little research or creative work. Fact finding was left to people elsewhere with the explanation that we were a poor state and could ill afford to engage in such advanced work. This also provided a convenient method of screening the discoveries which others were making and adopting only the new knowledge that would be most conducive to strengthening of the religious faith…"[48]

Olpin concluded by hailing improvements made during his era: creation of the graduate school; advances in mining operations, leading to local processing of raw materials; and government and world-affairs training of young people for foreign service. These revealed the necessary evolution of the University of Utah in the postatomic age, Olpin said.

"The University of Utah…is dedicated to the discovery, conservation and dissemination of knowledge, to the end that people everywhere may be saved. Those of us who comprise the cosmopolitan faculty and student body of this distinguished institution subscribe to the provincial faith of its founding fathers, that salvation is correlated with and dependent upon education. We shall seek to be guided by this concept as we move ahead in the Second Century of our State's history,"[49] Olpin promised. The state would remain provincial, he said, as long as nonconformers were suspect. He gave the speech to Salt Lake City's most prominent leaders of industry at a luncheon in the same downtown venue where he had made his convincing appeal to General Eisenhower for the transfer of Fort Douglas to the university.

CHAPTER 6

QUELLING THE MEDICAL CRISIS

Cosmopolitanism and provincialism, the opposing forces Olpin saw at the taproot of early Mormon attitudes toward schooling and the sources of the university's missionary zeal, were also evident in the evolution of an integrated University of Utah Medical Center. Olpin had little to do with hiring the faculty members who provided the medical training during his years at the university because the key appointments had already been made before he became president. But he had a firm conviction about the value of meeting problems head on, and challenges of a provincial nature plagued the training of medical professionals upon his arrival.

As had been the case with establishing the university's graduate school, there was considerable debate over whether the state could afford to provide education for future generations of medical professionals. Accreditors threatened to shut down the university's College of Medicine if improvements weren't made. After a preliminary accreditation visit to the four-year school in 1944, reviewers recommended more funds for research, increased space and equipment, improvement in some basic science departments, and removal of a few longtime professors.

The furor that followed attracted additional concern from the public. The university's Administrative Council had been organized to represent all faculty members before the University of Utah Board of Regents, and its members were deeply concerned that tenured faculty jobs were in jeopardy. The fact that the new medical-school department heads were to be paid at eight thousand dollars a year, whereas the top university salary in other departments was forty-five hundred dollars, also became a source of resentment. Some downtown doctors predicted that the new medical faculty members would make inroads into their private practices, and so they viewed prospective newcomers as threatening their professional income. Territoriality also fostered the attitude that providing only preclinical education was adequate, adding to the town-and-gown dispute.

Two months into his job, Olpin met with members of the medical faculty and practicing physicians. He told regents that he "was very concerned with the gossip which was indulged in at the meeting," and he set up a community-relations board to "better acquaint" members of the Utah Medical Association, the pharmaceutical association, hospitals, and the public with his plans to improve the medical program.[1] Three months later, Olpin convinced the Board of Regents to offer "the lucerne patch north and east of the Park Building"—a five-acre site near the campus hub—to house a state hospital to treat crippling diseases in children.[2] The idea had been in the works since 1944, stimulated by the inadequate facilities to care for four hundred cases of poliomyelitis. The Lions Clubs of the State of Utah, Utah Chapter of the National Foundation for Infantile Paralysis, and others promoted an interest in the development of a hospital for crippled children. The Utah legislature passed a bill appropriating $240,000 for the hospital's construction and $80,000 for operations in 1945. A citizens' board of trustees, chaired by mining engineer Clarence Bamberger, accepted the university's proposal to house the facility, and designs for both a fifty- and a one-hundred-bed children's polio hospital were commissioned.[3] The hospital was built on the university's new, upper-campus Medical Center site in 1949. Later, the state hospital for poliomyelitis and children's crippling diseases discontinued operation, and the building was given to the State Department of Health.

A campus plan envisioned a cluster of public and private hospitals with University Hospital at the center. The university's Board of Regents approached the LDS Church and the Shriners about building their hospitals on the campus. Decision makers at those hospitals were not receptive. President Olpin and Regent Sterling Sill met with LDS Church President George Albert Smith to see if the church's Primary Association would consider a university site for its future children's hospital.[4] However, the church found a site on Thirteenth Avenue, closer to the church-owned LDS Hospital. It was at Primary Children's Hospital that the medical school's training in pediatrics eventually took place under the direction of Utah College of Medicine graduate Dr. L. George Veasy, a pediatric cardiologist.

Meanwhile, the federal government paved the way for another type of affiliation when it determined that medical schools near veterans' hospitals should supervise attending physicians providing care.[5] A contract between the University of Utah and the Veterans Administration placed Salt Lake City's Twelfth Avenue VA hospital under the direction of College of Medicine Dean H. L. Marshall's committee. This group of faculty representatives were to nominate medical consultants for the hospital, who would then formulate medical policies and establish an educational program for the resident staff—several of whom would serve on a full-time basis at the VA.[6] In view of the state's meager financial support, Dean Marshall saw this as a welcome opportunity to earn nonstate support for the salaries of specialist consultants in pathology, radiology, and orthopedic surgery.

The dean had even bigger ideas to share, which he spelled out for Olpin in June 1946. They included planning a Medical Center northeast of the existing campus.

> May I call attention to a matter of which you are undoubtedly already aware? That is the desirability of working out a unified over-all plan for the development of the twenty acre campus tract intended for a Medical Center.
>
> If a model plan of development is arrived at now, and if each unit added conforms to this plan, public hospitals, and public health departments can be accommodated on that tract probably for the next 100 years. However twenty acres can be quickly dissipated by low buildings erected in disregard to a unified whole. Many universities are now working on model Medical Center plans, and…none of their locations is better than ours. Few are as good.
>
> Last November, purely on a personal basis, I discussed the long range planning of this tract as a medical center with the University Architect Taylor Wooley. He gave the problem some study and made some rough sketches. Possibly you have already taken official action along this line, which will influence the design, the material, and the exact location of the children's hospital….
>
> Two years ago I took representatives of the Rockefeller Foundation to this site. We sat at the eastern edge, looking westward over the site, and they both exclaimed that it was almost ideal. For a campus development of this sort, there is, I believe no doubt of federal and private philanthropic aid, which would, of course, not be forthcoming to an appendage of a politically controlled County Hospital. That point is well understood by certain individuals in local organized medicine and it is the basic reason for their opposition.[7]

The vice president of the Rockefeller Foundation, Allen Gregg, had been a classmate of previous dean Cyril Callister. Utah administrators put that relationship to their advantage because, as they said, "Gregg was high on Utah."[8] Still, there were local physicians who did not share the enthusiasm. Marshall supplied Olpin with details about these medical-school rivals, describing Dr. Ray T. Woolsey, president-elect of the Utah Medical Association, as their motivating force. Marshall said that, at the previous week's Medical Association meeting, Dr. Woolsey had "denounced this grandiose scheme of Dr. Marshall's for a Medical Center on the campus."[9] The source of the antagonism was obvious.

From 1905 to 1943, the university had offered basic medical-science courses to qualify students for the first two years of the standard four-year medical program. Graduates of the two-year preparatory program had to be accepted as transfer students at established medical schools in other parts of the country. These included Harvard, Johns Hopkins, Jefferson, Northwestern, and Louisville, where Utah's premedical students were frequently accepted. During the thirty-eight-year existence of the two-year school, 626 students completed the course and transferred.[10] But the growing trend to integrate the work of the two basic science years with the so-called clinical years was making the two-year school obsolete. Members of an accrediting committee noted that the entire area of the United States between the western edge of the Great Plains and the Pacific Coast and from the Canadian to the Mexican borders—a quarter of the entire nation—had just one doctor-training school. Medical education and research for this area's inhabitants were inadequately sustained by the "half school" at Utah. When the College of Medicine was threatened with reprisals for failure to keep pace with advances in academic medicine, Olpin's predecessor, President LeRoy Cowles, began plans for a four-year medical school. The urgent need for medical manpower during the war provided further stimulus for the university's medical program to grow.

The plan for a four-year College of Medicine had its detractors; many local medics energetically opposed the change. They asked university physicians to stipulate that they would not see private patients unless these patients first received a written referral from a downtown doctor. The full-time faculty adopted this conciliatory policy.

There was also the practical matter that there was no teaching hospital to provide clinical consultation. Salt Lake County commissioners made the Salt Lake County General Hospital available, making the professional care of patients a responsibility of the faculty of the College of Medicine. The county hospital consisted of an aging group of buildings that featured two operating rooms, no air conditioning, and somewhat-unreliable electrical and plumbing systems. Most patients were indigent and older, and most cases were emergencies. An infirmary provided two small wards for patients requiring long-term care. This facility did not offer the scope of practical training community doctors and specialists required.

In 1942 Dr. Cyril A. Callister, a local surgeon, was appointed half-time dean and set out to recruit a faculty for the new, four-year College of Medicine. Stanford polio expert and bacteriologist Dr. Louis P. Gebhardt was Callister's first appointee. After Gebhardt came Dr. Philip Price, head of surgery. He was the first medical-staff member appointed to the four-year College of Medicine. He came from Johns Hopkins University, the first modern medical school in the country. Since he had been born in Sinchang, China, to American Protestant missionaries, Price and his wife, Octavia Howard, a nurse, returned to China to work as medical missionaries before accepting the call to Utah.[11]

Price was largely responsible for recruiting his former colleague on the faculty at Johns Hopkins, Dr. Maxwell M. Wintrobe. These three key recruitments—Gebhardt, Price, and Wintrobe—plus the appointment of Dr. Louis S. Goodman from Yale University to head the Department of Pharmacology in 1944, all occurred before Olpin's return to Utah.

Three more Hopkins associates followed Wintrobe into the new frontier of Utah in the postwar years. All contributed to diversifying the faculty and broadened the range of thinking in their students. This new openness enriched the campus, giving it a more cosmopolitan atmosphere, an understanding of the aspirations of other peoples, and a personal identification with other cultures that could not be gained from textbooks.

Callister stepped down to make way for a full-time dean, and Olpin oversaw that search himself in 1946. Dr. Richard Young, former attending hematologist at Evanston, Illinois, and assistant to the dean at Northwestern Medical School, finally accepted the position in 1946. He was succeeded by Dr. Price, who became dean of the College of Medicine in 1955. Price was one of the Utah advisors in Ethiopia on the formation of medical training there.

The provincial habit that Olpin later noted in his Newcomen Society speech—referring to anyone who was not a Latter-day Saint as a gentile[12]—may have helped the fledgling medical school's recruitment. Doctors of the Jewish faith faced undisguised discrimination elsewhere. In 1930, when Dr. and Mrs. Wintrobe arrived in Baltimore from Tulane University in New Orleans, a Johns Hopkins department secretary gave them a list of possible apartments to rent. The secretary hastily withdrew the list and replaced it with another when she learned that the Wintrobes were Jewish. Prejudice was evident in very low quotas for Jewish students and Jewish department heads in many medical schools,[13] including Johns Hopkins, as Wintrobe observed in an oral history compiled by his colleague at Utah, Dr. Leonard Jarcho: "The atmosphere at Hopkins at that time was not the most salubrious one, shall we

This former barracks housed cancer research in the 1950s.

say. In many departments the attitude was a rather snobbish one, the right people in the main were the people who had the opportunities, who developed, who were promoted.... In fact, in some situations it was almost essential that one be a white Anglo-Saxon to get anywhere."[14]

Wintrobe told many others that, although he had arrived to find that his office would be an improvised one in the county infirmary, he felt confident that moving to Utah had kept his career from being shunted. The author of a key text in hematology, he carried with him a reputation that was important to Utah. If he had remained in Maryland, Wintrobe's promotion to assistant professor, he felt, was the highest rank he could expect to achieve. He was also serving as editor of the *Johns Hopkins Journal* with a combined salary of five thousand dollars per year. His starting salary of eight thousand dollars a year became a bone of contention at the University of Utah. Other departments compensated their faculty far less.

Dr. Louis Goodman was another prominent, pre-Olpin faculty member. He was senior author of a textbook on the pharmacological basis of therapeutics, which was used in more than 85 percent of the medical schools throughout the United States. The text was so popular that it was known as "the blue bible." To stretch the budget to hire Goodman, Cowles and Callister sought and gained a $25,000 gift from the Church of Jesus Christ of Latter-day Saints. The gift paid to outfit a pharmacology and physiology lab for the medical school, which was then housed in a red brick building that the army had built as a World War I dormitory barracks. It was just south of the Alfred C. Emery Building on President's Circle. Goodman brought with him contracted research grants totaling approximately $40,000, plus another five thousand dollars worth of laboratory equipment. From 1948 to 1968, Goodman's research on antiepileptic drugs was carried out through grants from the National Institutes of Health's National Institute of Neurological Disorders and Strokes.

The professional common denominator among these academic physicians was their collective dedication to the establishment of a first-rate school with a curriculum that would embrace excellence in teaching, research, and medical care. As Wintrobe succinctly phrased it, "the best academic climate is one where teaching and research are equal partners."[15] Cardiologist Hans Hecht, who directed the heart station at Salt Lake County General Hospital, was among those who credited Wintrobe with heading off crises. Problems he helped thwart stemmed from the political conditions occasionally damning operations and nearly causing Salt Lake County General Hospital to lose its accreditation. Although a succession of short-term deans at the medical school tended to weaken the structure, Wintrobe was a stabilizing influence.[16]

During this growth period, every full-time medical faculty member was expected to engage in original investigative work that would make him a better, more stimulating teacher. Conversely, every research worker was expected to participate in the teaching program, thus lending enrichment, interest, and perspective to his laboratory efforts. Olpin was for it—especially if their endeavors kept bright Utah students from going elsewhere to complete their medical and pharmacy degrees. The campus had only meager laboratory facilities. Medical faculty conducted research in both permanent and temporary buildings. Clinical services and training for medical students were five miles away at the Salt Lake County General Hospital, located at 2100 South and State Streets. A cavalry stable once used at Fort Douglas, the military post's old dental infirmary, and a two-story barracks building hauled eighty miles from Dugway Proving Ground also housed medical research projects.[17]

The stable was the site for a hundred-thousand-dollar muscular-dystrophy research project, headed by Dr. Wintrobe and geneticist Fayette Stephens. Senator Elbert D. Thomas orchestrated allocation of the grant. A former professor of political science at the university, Senator Thomas made a passionate plea that the U.S. Public Health Service (precursor to the National Institutes of Health) should direct all of the funds available in 1946 to the University of Utah to study heredity

Olpin holds the shovel as Regents break foothills ground on the Cancer Research Building circa 1950. It was the first building in what became the medical complex.

and crippling diseases. Congress had intended the funds to be divided. This was the first research grant to the College of Medicine, and it was renewed annually for thirty-one more years.[18]

The initial clinical report in 1946 of the impact of nitrogen mustard on Hodgkin's disease and other lymphomas evolved from studies of the effects of chemical-warfare agents. A cancer-research building erected near the foothills, also funded by the Public Health Service, was the first structure on the new Medical Center campus. It was dedicated in 1951. Adjacent and connecting to it was a two-hundred-thousand-dollar laboratory, which was constructed the following year and funded by the Atomic Energy Commission to study the cancerous effects of radiation. In 1952 the Veteran's Administration's medical services, overseen by university physicians, were united in a new hospital built on Foothill Boulevard. In 1954 the accreditation of Salt Lake County General Hospital by the American Medical Association Council on Medical Education was threatened. The College of Medicine was notified that its residency programs at the county hospital had not been approved.

It took Olpin eleven years to gain legislative approval to bring an end to these various makeshift medical arrangements. Olpin and Vice Presidents Elmo R. Morgan and G. Homer Durham accomplished that key step. With help from College of Medicine Dean Price, they secured from the state funds for planning

Dean and chief fund-raiser Dr. Kenneth B. Castleton, Salt Lake City Mayor Adiel F. Stewart, and philanthropist Maurice Warshaw represent community interests overseeing construction of the two-hundred-bed University Hospital beginning in July 1959. Many downtown doctors opposed a campus hospital.

and initial construction of classrooms, laboratories, and teaching and research facilities for a University Medical Center. They had to pledge not to ask the state legislature for more than four million toward the estimated ten million dollars in building costs for its construction. This time opposition centered on the Medical Center becoming a financial liability to the state. Price commented that since the medical school had received only $225,000 in appropriations over fifty years, it was high time the state invested a substantial sum for medical education.[19] His strategy was to parallel the proposed University Medical Center to the Geneva Steel Mill at Orem, near Provo. Neither would attempt to duplicate great structures in the East in size or cost, but instead would be well-planned, efficiently operated units suited to the area. College of Nursing and College of Medicine operation expenses would be held steady. Research would be funded by grants at no cost to the state. Hospital costs would be met largely or entirely by existing state and county welfare funds. The University Hospital would replace, rather than supplant, hospital beds and medical activities at the rundown Salt Lake County General Hospital.

Price used blue-collar vernacular to describe the vision that he and his colleagues shared for a new medical school and hospital building. He told elected officials this would be a trade in, not a brand-new vehicle: "What is envisioned here is not a luxury item, but a long-overdue necessity; not a fancy structure or a tourist-attraction, but a plain, highly functional service unit; something more nearly akin to a four-ton truck than to a chrome-trimmed limousine."[20]

This complex building would house not only the Colleges of Medicine and Nursing but also extensive research facilities for scientific work, a teaching and research hospital, outpatient and emergency departments, and a rehabilitation unit. Thus, it would help to prepare students for the type of medical practice needed in the community, including the care of seriously ill patients unlike those seen in typical community practices.

They touted the project's economic benefits. The medical college's 250 graduate and undergraduate students annually spent $750,000 in the state. Loss of accreditation due to poor facilities and programs could force those students out of Utah. With them would go the medical faculty. Poor facilities, Olpin said, hampered the university in multiple ways.

> In addition to classroom and general laboratory space shortages, we are limited in the number of new research grants which we can accept because we do not have the space to accommodate additional research activity. Restrictions of this kind could result in reduced opportunities for advanced graduate study.... As too many of our faculty members and students have regrettably come to know, facilities which were not ideal when they were "temporarily" acquired in 1948, have deteriorated. Major rehabilitation has not been undertaken because it was hoped we might avoid sizable expenditures on buildings which ought to be replaced. When the University acquired well over one hundred buildings of a wooden barracks-type construction, it was a mixed blessing.... they have been extremely expensive to maintain and we have begrudged every dollar put into them.[21]

Although a campus Medical Center had been talked about since 1943, official steps toward the realization of this dream did not begin until August 1955. Acting Dean Price wrote the University of Utah Board of Regents that the faculty believed the medical school had come to a critical juncture in its history and that it must either take a fresh step forward in its progress or else inevitably begin to lose ground. The faculty executive committee wanted the regents to adopt a formal resolution committing them to construct a Medical Center. The regents unanimously approved the ten-million-dollar Medical Center in 1956, charging the medical school to find ways and means of obtaining the money. Naysayers came forward to predict that ten million dollars could never be raised in a state with a population of only eight hundred thousand.[22] Again provincialism raised its head. Some physicians declared the Medical Center would be a "marble palace on a hill," and others wondered aloud why the facility couldn't be built on Salt Lake County General Hospital grounds.[23]

Four years of intensive planning went into the Medical Center structure, and the estimated cost for completion rose to fifteen million dollars. Administrators approached the federal government for research and training grants. The Health Facility Research branch of the National Institutes of Health allocated $2 million on the basis of a fifty-fifty match. Funds were contingent upon nonfederal sources contributing the remainder.[24] A committee of leading citizens was formed to organize a four-million-dollar fund-raising effort from corporations and businesses, philanthropic foundations, alumni, and friends of the university and medical school alike. Governor George D. Clyde broke ground on the Medical Center site driving an earth-moving excavator on January 9, 1962. Dr. Kenneth B. Castleton, a surgeon in private practice who had supervised one of the clinics at the old Salt Lake County General Hospital and a graduate of the university's two-year medical school, agreed to spearhead the community fund-raising campaign. He served as dean of the medical school from 1962 to 1969.

Under Castleton's leadership, the campaign for public contributions attracted gifts of unprecedented size and generosity. Especially noteworthy was the almost unanimous response of physicians in the state, who donated on average nearly a thousand dollars apiece to the project. This, Olpin noted proudly, bore "eloquent testimony to the growing importance of this institution in the life of the State, and the good relations that obtain between the College of Medicine and the public in general."[25]

Before the end of World War II, the only doctorates given by the university were 75 MD degrees from the College of Medicine. In the years of his presidency, Olpin signed 850 Doctor of Medicine diplomas. At his final commencement, June 8, 1964, 47 Doctors of Medicine graduated. Dean Castleton noted that the University of Utah College of Medicine, one of the nation's youngest, was still the only medical school between Denver and the Pacific Coast and Canada and Mexico. It had received continuous research grants from numerous sources but most notably from the National Institutes of Health. The faculty had begun to enjoy an international reputation, spread by leading textbooks written by College of Medicine professors in the fields of biochemistry, general medicine, hematology, and pharmacology. Their prominence was distinguished by four Markle scholarships, five Abel awards in pharmacology, four research awards in pediatrics, and

Olpin presided when the Medical Center's cornerstone was laid in 1962, but the hospital actually opened in 1965 during James C. Fletcher's administration.

thirteen research career-development awards. Two professorships were established through financial support from national voluntary health organizations in recognition of work building on the state's repository of family genealogical data and focused upon cardiovascular and neuromuscular disorders.

Half a decade later, the university's first vice president for medical affairs was appointed. He was Dr. Kenneth Castleton. Colleagues said that Castleton had sacrificed personal financial gain to secure support for the Medical Center, and Olpin told his daughter, Helen, that getting Castleton to agree to take the job had been one of his most significant achievements.[26] She also noted that for Olpin, who had lived in Japan and also worked on the atomic bomb, the reasons for the funding that brought Utah's environmental-medical research into prominence held personal significance. In proportion to its size, Utah received more American Cancer Society grants than any other state-assisted university.

Seven years elapsed from the time the first architectural drawings were rendered until the new University of Utah Medical Center was ready for occupancy. Grand opening of the University of Utah Medical Center was delayed beyond its scheduled July 1, 1964, time, and so its operation commenced during the administration of Olpin's successor, President James C. Fletcher. Its cornerstone was laid on October 8, 1962. On July 10, 1965, patients were moved from the county hospital to the university campus.

Chapter 7

Orchestrating the Arts

Olpin was not simply interested in creating a larger campus but a university of national and international stature that demonstrated a vital interest in enabling students to appreciate and enjoy the finer things of life. He also built an effective case that art must take its place alongside science before the world could work itself out of the many difficulties impeding its progress and threatening its existence. So it came to be that the University of Utah's present and future—and the present and future of the arts in Utah—rested on foundations and programs established under the determined artistic leadership of a distinguished scientific researcher.

Olpin accomplished this task largely by concentrating on the campus a combination of artists/faculty members, performing organizations, and professional and academic curricula designed to produce capable *and* cultivated human beings. While carrying out what he felt was his duty to nurture the arts, Olpin also drew flak when cutting-edge performances and exhibits caused conservative audiences to question whether university programs adequately represented their community's moral and aesthetic values.

As artists, LeRoy J. Robertson, Alvin Gittins, Maurice Abravanel, and Willam F. Christensen were attracted to a dynamic campus that was opened up to them. College of Fine Arts administrator Lowell M. Durham described Olpin as creating a unique minirenaissance of the arts in Utah, a "re-awakening…unparalleled in the cultural annals of Western America."[1]

92

President Olpin made a bold offer to Maurice Abravanel to house and showcase the Utah Symphony on campus.

G. Homer Durham describes the atmosphere in more detail in his essay, "The Close of the First Century": "New, pulsating vitality, even controversy, was evident as the University Theatre came to represent not only community interests and aspirations, but also scholarly, inquisitive, searching dramatic pieces. To this by 1950 was added the Summer Festival, the Ballet Theater, and opera in dimension never before experienced in Utah. The Departments of Music, Speech and Theatre, with their kindred, combined in many ways to produce a cultural renaissance."[2]

Olpin was the catalyst for a unique campus/community relationship that brought standing-room-only crowds to the university and firmly established its role in incorporating music, the arts, and the humanities into the life of the community. He hired a major composer, Robertson, as chairman of the Department of Music on the heels of the music professor's attention-getting receipt of the twenty-five-thousand-dollar Henry Reichhold Prize in the Symphony of the Americas contest in 1947. At a crucial time in its infancy, he invited the Utah Symphony under music director and conductor Maurice Abravanel to make its home on the campus in 1948. This enriched the music faculty and made professional opera and oratorio possible, where glee-club choruses had been the university's previous musical forté. Summer-festival productions of opera and musicals combined the

The University Theatre Ballet, Utah Symphony, and forty-eight-voice university chorus performed Summer Festivals outdoors in the stadium. This 1964 production of Faust starred singer Glade Peterson.

forces of the Utah Symphony, University Theatre, and ballet. These were "artistic successes and financial failures" directed by C. Lowell Lees, chairman of the university Department of Speech (which at the time included theater).[3] New, pulsating vitality, even controversy, was evident as the University Theatre came not only to represent community interests and aspirations but also to stage scholarly, inquisitive, searching dramatic pieces. To this schedule by 1950 was added the Summer Festival, the Ballet Theater, and opera in dimensions never before experienced in Utah. The Departments of Music and Speech and Theatre, with their kindred, combined in many ways to produce a cultural renaissance.[4]

Between 1948 and 1965, hundreds of thousands of students and community members enjoyed the outdoor spectacles, and their popularity made Lees and Olpin anxious to have a professional choreographer on campus, who could train students to perform the dances. Olpin also headed the initiative to construct a replica of the old Salt Lake Theatre on campus. And the president personally oversaw the negotiation with donors over artwork and the display of fine art in a museum above his own Park Building office. The arts in the university's Olpin era were richly endowed. The university became a cultural, as well as an educational, community center.

In the spring of 1953, one of the most noteworthy cultural events was the premiere of Robertson's *Oratorio from the Book of Mormon,* presented in collaboration with Maurice Abravanel and the Utah Symphony and the university's combined choruses. The musical work, which attracted national attention and was recorded and released by Vanguard records in 1961, was heard by eighteen thousand people during its five performances. Robertson had headed the music department at Brigham Young University from 1925 to 1948.

Before wooing Robertson, Olpin had tried to hire Lorin F. Wheelwright, a composer of LDS hymns and supervisor of music for Utah schools, to fill the vacancy to head the university's Department of Music. Wheelwright felt that his job was too important to give up but suggested that the president hire Robertson instead. Olpin announced Robertson's appointment at the last in a series of six "at-home" programs in the Student Union. The news drew enthusiastic applause from those who had gathered to hear a concert by the university's symphony orchestra. Olpin also announced that day that Lowell M. Durham, a lecturer in the Department of Music and critic for the *Salt Lake Tribune,* would become secretary of the university's College of Fine Arts. Durham, he said, would coordinate administrative details, including sculpture, painting, drama, dance, and music.

Olpin crafted a tentative agreement with officials of the Utah State Symphony Orchestra Association that would permit the orchestra to perform twenty concerts a year under the auspices of the university in Kingsbury Hall.[5] He also announced that the Department of Music would work closely with the Utah Symphony conducted by Maurice Abravanel, which would rehearse on campus. Abravanel became another of the University's "dollar-a-year men" and was appointed full professor in 1949. Most importantly, according to Durham, the disheartened musicians in the Utah Symphony went from practicing in freezing labor-union halls or at the Boys and Girls Club and the Eagles Lodge to playing in a remodeled barracks in the former Fort Douglas, where they felt more comfortable and welcome for the next ten years.

The move, Durham said, was a godsend to both Abravanel and the university's music students: "The important thing from the Music Department's point of view was its availability to students to sit in on rehearsals, to walk through and see really what professional music is all about. In addition to that the Utah Symphony's principal artists, about ten to twelve of them, were made adjunct faculty members...."

The Department of Architecture, headed by Roger Bailey, was housed in a barracks embellished by the dean.

The greatest thing that you have is a professional orchestra on your campus. No one will really appreciate that until it is gone."[6]

Abravanel's association with the University of Utah began ambitiously with the school's combined choruses, including four hundred voices, collaborating with an eighty-member orchestra to perform Beethoven's difficult Roman Catholic mass *Missa Solemnis* in Kingsbury Hall in December 1948. His tenure lasted for thirty-two years, with the Tabernacle in Temple Square becoming Abravanel's primary podium. In tribute to the symphony/university affiliation, he conducted Brahms's *Academic Festival Overture* eight times. Adding the symphony's principals to the university's faculty meant that musical-performance students could complete their educations at Utah without having to move to New York or Los Angeles, where there were established music conservatories. A special performance degree, the Master of Musical Arts, was devised for vocal and instrumental students. Ph.D.s were awarded to several students who composed scores as their dissertations.

The year before Robertson became chair of the Department of Music, sculptor Avard Fairbanks had been named the first dean of the College of Fine Arts, and the school was accorded the right to offer graduate degrees. This sharply increased the number of candidates for advanced degrees and the satisfactory completion of their work within the next five years. In the almost sixty years since its establishment, the Department of Fine Arts had conferred a total of nine graduate degrees. Between 1947 and 1952, the new College of Fine Arts granted forty. Besides increased enrollment in graduate programs, some undergraduate curricula—notably in music, painting, and ballet—were augmented to accommodate the higher requirements of graduate entrance examinations, as well as extend the range of available instruction to promising students. This was the result of executive decisions by Olpin, who, according to business vice president Paul Hodson, was especially focused on the new schools of fine arts, pharmacy, nursing, and architecture, as well as the separation of the colleges of mining and engineering and the expansion of the medical school.[7]

Fairbanks had come from Michigan, as had the head of the Department of Architecture, Roger Bailey. The university's Department of Architecture, housed originally in the basement of the Park Building and begun by Bailey in 1949, offered the only accredited Bachelor of Architecture degree in the intermountain area. Architecture was part of the College of Fine Arts, and this caused a great deal of tension between Fairbanks and Bailey, who disliked each other intensely. Throughout the 1950s, Fairbanks reported his side of their frequent squabbles to Olpin on a regular basis. Many of his complaints centered on what he felt was a corrupting influence: modernism. He equated it with Communism as a subversive movement: "The corruption of art students' principles stems from being exposed to foreign art manglers, the subversive doctrine of [-]isms, Communist-inspired and Communist connected. These influencers have one boasted goal: the destruction of our cultural tradition and priceless heritage."[8]

Olpin instructed Durham to perform the duties of a shadow dean: attending to administrative tasks so that Robertson could compose and Fairbanks wouldn't have to manage people. The Master of Architecture degree in the College of Fine Arts was approved in the fall of 1960. Durham was chief administrative officer of the Department of Music for sixteen years. In 1954 he was promoted to dean of the College of Fine Arts, and Fairbanks was demoted to consultant in fine arts and resident sculptor.

Durham claimed he hired painter Alvin Gittins, who, despite a lack of academic degrees, helped to professionalize a "shambles of an art department."[9] To a department that also included painters LeConte Stewart and Mabel Frazer, Durham successfully lobbied to add V. Douglas Snow, a University of Utah theater major who had gone on to earn two degrees in fine art at the Cranbrook Academy of Art in Michigan. Snow was teaching at Wayne State University in Detroit when the University of Utah finally offered him a position in 1954. Snow and

Painter V. Douglas Snow, pictured here in 1964, was part of the Department of Art's modern movement.

Gittins—portrait painter, art professor, and department chair from 1957 to 1963, brought in outstanding contemporary artists and exposed the Department of Art to major modern influences—particularly abstract expressionism.

From 1933 on, annual student and Utah art exhibits were held in the Student Union, which later became the Music Building and was located near University Street. Department of Art faculty and student members of the Union board managed these exhibitions. The Park Building also had an art gallery, known since 1916 as the art gallery for the state, where works in the university's permanent collection were displayed on the fourth floor. The art comprising the collection in 1940 was worth an estimated $836,106 in 2006 dollars, and that is likely an underestimate of its value, according to Utah Museum of Fine Arts historian Ron Allen, who points out that undervaluing art inventory was the norm with state agencies faced with insurance premiums and price inflation during the 1940s.[10] The Park Building gallery was open for visitors daily, but due to limited space and student traffic, exhibitions took place in the Student Union, which became a Department of Art annex.

Avard Fairbanks sculpted a symbol of Ute pride. However, his frequent complaining caused Olpin to release him as dean of the College of Fine Arts.

The top floor of the Park Building was remodeled into a gallery and became the Utah Museum of Fine Arts, featuring the Hudnut Collection.

Shortly after his appointment in 1946, Olpin began negotiating with Mrs. Winifred Kimball Hudnut about donating her substantial collection of art to the University of Utah. A native Utahn, Mrs. Hudnut lived in New York and was the widow of Richard Hudnut, a perfume and cosmetics magnate. Olpin went east to convince her to keep the collection together by displaying it at the University of Utah. He claimed that she told him his appearance in New York was most timely: "When I arrived at Mrs. Hudnut's home I discovered that she had, just the day before, authorized the auctioning of her collection."[11] She reiterated that she wanted the European treasures that she and her husband had collected to be the basis of a fine-arts museum, and though a gallery already existed at the University of Utah, Olpin gave her the impression that the expanded and remodeled art gallery that reopened in the Park Building in 1951 was actually new. Olpin had tried, but failed, to get the legislature to approve funds to build a new, stand-alone museum.

The Department of Art, which had overseen the gallery, had moved out of the Park Building into a temporary barracks acquired from Salt Lake City, and Olpin, tired of the quarreling between art and architecture faculty, had appointed his friend I. Owen Horsfall, a mathematician, internationalist, and director of the Extension Division, as half-time curator of the Utah Museum of Fine Arts. The president still made a round-the-clock job out of meeting with decorators, arranging to have a freight elevator installed to move works into place, corresponding with donors, and attending art-museum meetings and openings. He went to New

York expressly to tell Mrs. Hudnut that if she donated her collection, the university would house it. He invited her personally to install furnishings and arrange the French room in the museum.

At roughly the same time, Olpin began negotiating with L. Boyd Hatch, a Utahn and successful New York City financier, who also was considering donating a major collection to the University of Utah. Hatch and Olpin agreed that the Hudnut collection should be secured and installed first, and Olpin was disappointed when the university's Board of Regents refused to authorize fund-raising to construct an Elizabethan period room to house the furnishings. On Monday, May 7, 1951, the public was invited to the opening of the seventy-five-hundred-square-foot gallery/museum—the former attic of the Park Building. It encompassed the entire fourth floor, and in the early 1950s, more donors came forward with rare tapestries, furnishings, and artwork.

Still, the Board of Regents did not wish to be seen as investing in luxuries over necessities. "While discussing this matter it was very much apparent that the new Board of Regents will be actuated by a desire to effect economies and that they will look upon education as a means to earning a living or a practical approach to the problems, and the cultural things are rather far from their thinking. Clearly the professions and other areas of study which will provide people for earning a livelihood will take place over courses designed to teach people the value of living," wrote Olpin in his journal.[12]

The following spring, the Anne McQuarrie Hatch Room, including forty-eight contributed works of art, was opened in a formal reception.[13] Five days earlier the university's Board of Regents had officially changed the name of the gallery to the Utah Museum of Fine Arts.[14] The art museum's collection included paintings by European masters dating from the Renaissance, pieces of furniture from seventeenth- and eighteenth-century France, a room of old English and Tudor furnishings, many ancient jade figurines from China, and the Egyptian objects donated by Aziz S. Atiya.

Olpin continued serving as the de-facto director of the Utah Museum of Fine Arts and drew criticism from students and faculty for his role in what became known as the "Union Building Art Scandal" of 1961. Panels set up in the hallway opposite the main ballroom in the new Student Union exhibited student artwork, which that year included charcoal sketches of seminude figures. After some visitors complained that a group of Eagle Scouts attending a banquet there had been exposed to nudity, the Board of Regents directed Gittins to have the offending panels removed.[15]

Art exhibits were frequently featured in the new Student Union, designed by Provo architect Fred Markham.

Visitors enjoy an exhibition of Japanese art and crafts at the University of Utah Student Union in 1959.

To *Daily Utah Chronicle* editor Ernie Ford, Olpin lamented that by exerting "certain freedom of choice," a few members of the fine-arts faculty had offended their peers:

> In the art field, the professors or art and the students wish to impose their type of art on the people, even though the other sixty-four or sixty-five departments are unhappy about this single department having such a front window in which to display the product of their efforts. Academic freedom means one thing to one person and another to another person and there is the question of good judgment or poor judgment, good taste or poor taste. I pointed out to Ernie Ford that there were places on this campus where you could go and see people dissecting human bodies, removing genital parts or other limbs and certainly there was no objection to this, but if this action were taking place down on the corner of Main Street where the passerby could watch it, there would be plenty of protest and we would be required to discontinue such an operation in that place. The display of art is somewhat the same. If people want to go see it, that is fine, but one cannot place it as an obstacle which people cannot get by to get in the building and then not use good taste in the selection of the art that is displayed.[16]

University officials said that the display panels obstructed the free flow of travel through the building and that future student art would be exhibited elsewhere. Students published their objections to such censorship in the *Daily Utah Chronicle*. Controversy snowballed.

The "Union Building Art Scandal" erupted in 1961 when protesters decried removal of a nude portrait in a student art exhibit. Olpin said exhibitions at the Student Union posed a fire hazard and should take place elsewhere.

Olpin took the position that he hadn't objected to the display of nude portraiture, but rather that Student Union passersby were unknowingly subjected to it. Let them paint what they wish, he said, but don't obligate others to see it. Publicity over the banishment of the nude sketches finally caused Olpin to ask the Faculty Committee on Academic Freedom and Tenure to review whether his actions were stifling free speech on campus.[17] Administrator Sydney W. Angleman, director of general education, responded that the Park Building location for the Utah Museum of Fine Arts was too far from students' beaten path to get their attention. He argued that no place on campus provided students the "day-by-day, readily accessible experience in art" that the main corridor of the Union Building did. Minimizing wide exposure to contemporary art would also have a deleterious effect on student artists, he lamented, and he encouraged the Board of Regents to reconsider its decision to prohibit student art displays in the Student Union.[18]

Officers of the Sons of Utah Pioneers meet with LDS Church President David O. McKay and university officials to plan the campaign to build Pioneer Memorial Theatre in 1961.

Letters both supporting Olpin's judicious stand, and opposing his intolerance, kept the matter alive in the newspaper's public forum for several weeks.

Three years before the scandal over nude art, Olpin had withstood more-private criticism from Hugh C. Smith, president of a Los Angeles County, California, stake of the Church of Jesus Christ of Latter-day Saints, who had complained that the fourth annual Institutional [Art] Exhibition was part of a Communist conspiracy. The nine modern American artists whose work had been displayed by the Department of Art included four who had been compelled to testify in House and Senate investigations of un-American activities in 1948 and 1949. They were painters Stuart Davis, Jack Levine, Ben Shahn, and Max Weber. Smith told Olpin he could not, in good conscience, recommend that fine American boys and girls attend the University of Utah if its faculty's views were not in harmony with the United States government's constitutional principles.[19]

Smith also sent a copy of his objections to Joseph Fielding Smith, who was then president of the LDS Church's Quorum of the Twelve Apostles. Gittins penned a defensive letter where he noted that both Brigham Young University and Utah State University at Logan had longer histories of teaching modern art than the University of Utah did. Olpin forwarded it to David O. McKay, president of the LDS Church, on October 27, 1958, "in case the allegations prompting these letters come to your attention."[20] Beyond acknowledging receipt of Olpin's and Gittins's letters, McKay apparently never took up the matter with Olpin.

Arriving at the dedication of Pioneer Memorial Theatre in October 1962 are, left to right, Paul Hodson, David L. McKay, LDS Church President David O. McKay, Leland B. Flint, and J. Willard Marriott Sr.

McKay and Olpin had already had many communications over the university's construction, and the church's funding, of a replica of the old Salt Lake Theatre on the university campus—a decision recommended by the Utah Centennial Commission, chaired by President McKay, and endorsed by the Board of Regents in 1946. But the project was a legacy from the Cowles administration. Many university officials felt that any cultural renaissance in the state must include rebuilding this historic monument, but the architecture and building specifications had to be painstakingly negotiated with the LDS Church.[21]

For the theater really to become a cultural asset, university officials felt it must include actor training, as well as provide wholesome entertainment to the city and state. In 1957 Kennecott Copper Corporation made a $250,000 donation, the LDS Church contributed $325,000, and the State of Utah appropriated $500,000 toward the erection of the $1.5-million Pioneer Memorial Theatre. It was 1962 when the building was finally dedicated—a hundred years after the dedicatory prayer offered at the opening of the original Salt Lake Theatre on March 6, 1862. Shakespeare's *Hamlet* was the opening production.

Olpin was also the driving force behind the creation of a Department of Ballet at the University of Utah, the first one established at an American university, which set a pattern for other institutions to follow. Willam F. Christensen, a Brigham City native who had returned to Utah in 1949 to choreograph the Summer Festival production in the university stadium, headed it. Christensen was already a recognized pioneer in the world of dance, having cofounded the San Francisco Ballet Company. After two more successful summer seasons, Olpin offered Christensen the position of professor of ballet with the charge to begin a ballet school under the aegis of the Department of Theatre and Speech. Christensen had told Olpin he did not want to teach as part of the physical-education program.

This caused an uproar in the Department of Health, Physical Education, and Recreation, where the faculty overseeing the physical education of women strongly objected to the teaching major and the professional major in dance being separated under two different administrative heads. They complained to Olpin and the Board of Regents that College of Fine Arts Dean Avard Fairbanks had already made Elizabeth Hayes, a Ph.D. in the physical-education department, head of dance; that Hayes and Christensen could not agree on "their basic philosophy of art and of the teaching of dance" (hers, modern; his, classical); and that it would be unfair to train students in the classical ballet tradition when there were no jobs for professional dancers.[22]

The University Theatre Ballet, created in 1952, did give students the opportunity to perform for the community. The University Theatre and Ballet Theater each presented a series of major programs and attracted wide audiences. Only three years after its creation, the University Theatre Ballet and the Utah Symphony combined talents in 1955 to present *The Nutcracker.* Abravanel, Christensen said, was the one who wanted to perform Tchaikovsky's fairy ballet. The University Theatre manager predicted the performance would flop if it was held between Christmas and New Year's Day because no one would come to see it. Christensen said that he had thought about moving the performance to the Capitol Theatre, but Olpin wanted it on campus, and so he sent a crew with hammers to dig a pit for the orchestra in Kingsbury Hall.

As the scope and abilities of the University Theatre Ballet grew, so did its aspirations. In 1963 Christensen, with support from arts patron Glenn Walker Wallace, successfully applied for a Ford Foundation grant of $175,000 to establish the Utah Civic Ballet.[23] As the successor to the University Theatre Ballet and the first fully professional ballet company in the Intermountain West, the new company toured the region for the next several years, gaining a strong following in Utah's surrounding states. Unlike Abravanel, whose university/symphony collaboration ended in 1968 when the orchestra left campus, Christensen never abandoned his interest in teaching. He persuaded the university to allow him to move his "private" bal-

Willam F. Christensen returned to Utah to teach ballet, including choreographing the University Theatre Ballet in staging The Nutcracker in Kingsbury Hall.

let school to campus, inaugurating a conservatory program where students were trained from the age of eight.

Olpin's most formative job instilled in him a lifelong passion for television. On April 7, 1927, A. Ray Olpin had played an active role in the historic first public transmission of a television image by the Bell Telephone Company. He was placed in charge of the television equipment at the radio station in Whippany, New Jersey, about twenty miles from New York City. Other facilities had been set up in Washington, D.C. Herbert Hoover, secretary of commerce at the time, spoke in Washington, using a telephone line, and was seen and heard by a gathering of three hundred editors and reporters in New York. Then Olpin appeared and gave a brief explanation of the new electronic system. The same guests heard and saw him. This was the beginning of wireless television, and Olpin was one of the first three people ever to appear on a television screen.

Those who saw the demonstration were so enthusiastic about its possibilities that President Walter S. Gifford of the Bell Telephone Company felt that he should provide a word of caution. He told the gathered crowd not to mortgage their homes to buy stock in any television companies that might be organized then, stating that television was a reality but would "pause on the threshold of economic possibility" for a couple of decades.[24] This proved to be true, but Olpin's enthusiasm for television multiplied when he thought about using it to stretch teaching resources.

Soon after the television exhibition, Olpin participated in developing photo-electric cells that had a spectral response similar to that of the human eye. Later, he invented cells that responded well to yellow and green light, and others that reacted to red and infrared light. Using cells that responded primarily to blue light, the researchers found it possible to transmit images in color, and television in natural color became a reality. When the "icono phone," or visual telephone, was developed, Olpin actively participated in the initial demonstrations.

Among his first announcements after his return to Utah was the hope of establishing educational television. He described the new medium as opening innovative highways to the mind. The way he brought KUED, Channel 7, into existence before educational television reached most areas of the United States is another epic diplomatic feat. He negotiated with the Federal Communications Commission (FCC) in 1946, building the case that rural Utahns sorely needed access to the instructional programs originating on the University of Utah campus. Wary of the growing popularity of television with theater—and movie—audiences, Kingsbury Hall Manager Gail Plummer urged Olpin to apply to the FCC for a Salt Lake City–area broadcast-station license.[25]

There was no financing available for this kind of cultural programming; Utah's resources were stretched (as always) to the breaking point. An educational television bill that would have contributed $250,000 toward realizing the potential of educational television suffered a familiar fate: veto by Governor J. Bracken Lee. Lee made the case that buildings and facilities to handle the university's existing educational program must come before broadcasted material.[26]

With his usual ingenuity, Olpin learned of a Ford Foundation grant of a hundred thousand dollars, available only if it could be matched. He persuaded the foundation to let him match those funds with equipment in lieu of money. As a gift from commercial television station KDYL-TV, the university acquired its old broadcasting antennae. Olpin convinced the foundation staff to accept the tower as matching funds.

Eventually KUED was established in 1958 under Olpin's personal direction: the president strongly believed that through educational television, the university could find an even-wider audience while contributing to quality programming. Uncontrolled television, he cautioned, had the capacity to become an "atomic

Olpin shepherded KUED-TV into being. Educational television was among his favored projects.

bomb of ideas" that could destroy viewers.[27] He also called it the air battle for men's minds.[28]

KUED went on the air on January 20, 1958. Olpin himself chose the call letters KUED: *K* as a station west of the Mississippi, *U* for Utah and the University of Utah, and *E* and *D* for education. Early programs on KUED included *U and Culture,* a weekly show featuring the College of Fine Arts; French and Russian language projects, the latter made possible by a grant from the National Defense Education Act; a postgraduate medical-education series aired nationally; and a series of presentations clarifying the issues facing education in Utah, for which KUED received the national School Bell Award for 1960. The Adult Education Center at Ann Arbor, Michigan, under the sponsorship of the Fund for Adult Education, financed by the Ford Foundation, provided most of the programs broadcast during the first decade at KUED. Still, the university can make a significant claim to the origins of educational television, and some historians question whether Utah's Philo T. Farnsworth or A. Ray Olpin should be rightfully called "the father of TV."

A great outpouring of creative activity in the arts got under way at the University of Utah with the end of World War II, and this may well have been the tangible expression of repressed desires. Some credited Elva Olpin, A. Ray's wife, with infecting him with a passion for music that had a way of shaping and carrying old dreams to new heights. She was a brash soprano, and theirs was a musical home. Others decided simply that pioneering seeds that had been well planted now came to full flower.[29]

At the end of Olpin's administration, Dean Lowell Durham stepped down, making way for the appointment of painter Ed Maryon as acting dean of the College of Fine Arts. That year the administration of the Utah Museum of Fine Arts passed under the supervision of the College of Fine Arts. After many years of occupying temporary buildings, the Departments of Art and Architecture prepared to move, with the university Museum of Fine Arts, into a $3.5-million Fine Arts Center.[30]

Olpin took in stride challenges that presidents of universities in less-conservative communities might never face: defending controversial artists and educating regents about the role of a state's flagship university. Daniel J. Dykstra, a former academic vice president, saw Olpin this way: "Every facet of the University program had his interest and support. If this meant, as it did, that he seldom missed attending a football or basketball game, it also meant that he seldom missed a concert, a play, or a lecture. It was difficult for him to accept the fact that a concert, a play or a lecture sponsored by the University was ever below par."[31]

Olpin contributed to professionalization and heightened proficiency by enhancing the technical resources available to prospective painters, architects, sculptors, dancers, actors, composers, and radio-TV technicians and so became recognized as a patient godfather of the postwar arts in Utah.

CHAPTER 8

RECALLING OLPIN'S LEGACY

Universities are accustomed to a metronomic pace. Coursework is divided into terms: summer, winter, spring, and fall. Each fall a new class enters. Each spring a convocation marks the awarding of degrees. There is a time to prepare the annual budget, a time to bill students' tuition, and a time to mark grades. Regularity is the lifeblood of a campus. Turning points can rarely be predicted. In an important time in the University of Utah's history, A. Ray Olpin's leadership and research experience and the GI Bill of Rights coincided to set a faster tempo, resulting in a period of enormous growth and progress.

Olpin's endurance at the helm for eighteen and a half years is one of the reasons that historians today, as well as faculty who served in his administration, have for decades spoken of "the Olpin years" as definitive ones for the University of Utah. By contrast the average term for a university president in his era was five and a half years. Olpin did more than endure, however; he faced head on the deficits that were evident after the war. The University of Utah was badly underbudgeted when he arrived. But the president pressed heavily on the state legislature to increase the institutional budget, and he was successful.

He served during a time of suspicion and distrust. The atomic bomb, the cold war, and Sputnik had a particularly profound effect upon universities, which were expected to unite science and industry to secure America's moral and economic competitive edge. Because there were so few universities between the Mississippi and West Coast, the University of Utah was expected to take a prominent role in furthering research and extending knowledge. It became a significant force in the scientific and engineering enterprises of the nation. This was an historic time, and Olpin rose to the occasion. During his administration, funding for research grew from $200,000 to $6 million. He had a clear idea of the way federal grants could stimulate a golden age at a research university.

A. Ray Olpin's personal intervention with General Eisenhower allowed the university to acquire at little cost part of old Fort Douglas for permanent campus expansion. This brought the university's land holdings from 150 to more than 600 acres. The university refurbished the land and buildings for students. They housed worldwide athletes competing in the 2002 Winter Olympic Games; the campus was their Olympic Village.

Some lament that the university gained property at the expense of the army reservists who had trained there.[1] Nevertheless, the historic red-brick and white-trimmed quarters, plus new dormitories that were built to the east and south of the parade grounds and officers' circle, have established a living/learning environment connecting the present and the past beneath glorious trees. Combined, the campuses above and below Fort Douglas Boulevard are nostalgic and contemporary. Now there are essentially two Student Unions: the one Olpin had built in 1957 and the Chase N. Peterson Heritage Center in Fort Douglas, which opened in 2000. The Student Union on lower campus provides computer and copying services, a cafeteria, and a bowling alley for students who commute from far and near. Heritage Commons is home base for thirty-five hundred students living in campus residence halls. The building on President's Circle that served as the Student Union during the war years has been remade into a music building and concert hall. A replica of Maestro Maurice Abravanel's study is housed there, and this also connects visitors to Olpin's legacy of furthering music education through the risky proposition he made to the Utah Symphony.

One of Olpin's last official duties was presiding at the dedication of Pioneer Memorial Theatre. He took the opportunity to recap his presidential balancing act. The LDS Church had made funding for the theatre possible, but Olpin and the Department of Theatre wanted to assert that actors trained there would be free to exercise their academic freedom. The university needed state money to build the theatre, but the state didn't have the money, and the legislature didn't want to bond the project. The two struck a rare pay-as-you-go agreement, and the University got the green light on the project. At the ribbon-cutting ceremony, Olpin unveiled an oil portrait of the LDS Church's ninth President, David O. McKay, by Department of Art Chair Alvin Gittins. Olpin recalled the debate over recreating a likeness of the old Salt Lake Theatre on campus during tight financial times:

I told the story of President McKay's lack of interest in building a replica…how the campaign got off the ground, how J. Bracken Lee and the Board of Examiners had incurred the wrath of state legislators when they made a deficit appropriation of a half million dollars to match a half million contributed jointly by Kennecott and the LDS Church, and how President McKay had come up to a meeting of the legislators, state, and city officials, Chamber of Commerce people, and so on in the Governor's Board Room, and as he walked into the crowded room, he broke into a smile and said he had come to confess his sins. From that moment on the whole purpose of the meeting seemed to be to work out an arrangement whereby the legislature, which was soon to convene under a new governor, did make an appropriation to offset the deficit of a half-million dollars.[2]

Olpin was tenacious in aligning disparate interests. In the end, and largely due to the support of the university's Board of Regents, he managed to win over axe-wielding Governor Lee. A. Ray and Elva Olpin and Margaret and J. Bracken Lee ended up taking a tour of the Orient together after Olpin retired and Lee had been elected mayor of Salt Lake City. Lee expressed his fondness for the Olpins in a personal note, dated December 16, 1968, which he mailed to their home in the St. Mary's neighborhood of Salt Lake City.

Dear Ray:

Although I write many letters throughout the year, I always look forward with pleasure to the opportunity of writing you to let you know how much I appreciate your friendship and enjoy our association.

Margaret and I were especially delighted that we were able to join with you on our recent tour of the Orient and you certainly helped make our trip the success it was. We feel privileged to count you and Mrs. Olpin among our good friends.

Margaret joins with me in expressing our sincere best wishes to you and your loved ones for a Christmas filled with much happiness and a New Year of peace and joy.

Sincerely yours,
Bracken[3]

Talk about furthering person-to-person understanding through experience in foreign countries! Olpin had always done that.

During his administration, the campus quadrupled in size. Many of the buildings today were built under Olpin's supervision. He started a ten-year construction program where thirty buildings were completed, including Milton Bennion Hall, the Merrill Engineering Building, and, of course, the A. Ray Olpin Student Union. The facilities were needed to accommodate unprecedented demand for new academic programs. Utah went from a state of hardscrabble miners extracting low-grade copper and wool growers sheering sheep to a place where its university had to fulfill the promise of new vitality for the state, the nation, and the world.

Early in his career Olpin turned the lucerne pasture behind the Park Building over to a community group to construct a children's polio hospital. But the vision of the way the medical school could best serve the region's needs extended Olpin's expectations just as the advent of television extended ours. The polio hospital wasn't built on lower campus. It became part of a new, upper medical campus. And Olpin presided at the groundbreaking of the University Medical Center there, too.

Olpin was ambitious by nature, and he had opportunities to shorten his stay. In 1963, the year before he retired, he spent March through May in Japan and the Philippines on a Ford Foundation grant to study educational television. Afterward he gave a personal, informal report to Vice President Richard M. Nixon. He could have furthered his career at Washington State College in Pullman, where he was offered the presidency in 1951. Or he might have gone back into industry. Officials with the Sugar Association tried to hire him as president. Such a move would have been consistent with his platform opposing the export of raw materials from Utah. With his background in developing new textile production methods and his training at Bell Laboratories, Olpin might have advanced the processing of sugar beets. However, he said that leaving the university would have betrayed those whom he had hired.

Something in Olpin inspired a ceaseless devotion to the University of Utah. When the time came for him to prepare for his retirement, he requested the title, "emeritus president." He wanted to keep an office on campus so that he could continue serving the university—even as an unpaid representative. Olpin tried to retire when he was sixty-two. The Board of Regents persuaded him to stay on. Then community boosters wanted him to head the Promote Utah Foundation, but there were no funds for the project. He believed in Utah. He believed in science. He believed in the opportunity that a University of Utah education provided to build better citizens.

When Olpin accepted the presidency at Utah, he had no place to live. When he stepped down from his seven-day-a-week job to retire into academic reflection, his successors couldn't find a suitable place on campus for him to do his work. He wound up in a School of Business office, working on his memoirs.

Olpin helped the university grow up in so many ways, and this had a profound effect. His goal from the outset was to make the institution a true university, mature and fully functioning. It was he who called 1946 to 1964 the University of Utah's years of promise.

Notes

Chapter 1
Putting the Pieces into Place

1. Colonel K. D. Nichols, postcard to A. Ray Olpin, December 28, 1945, Olpin Presidential Records, box 2, University Archives, University of Utah, Salt Lake City (hereafter cited as University Archives).

2. Elinore Partridge, interview with A. Ray Olpin, January 9, 1975, Salt Lake City, notes in author's possession.

3. A. Ray Olpin, "Birth and Name," "My Daily Journal," vol. 5 (1920), pp. 1–6, copy in author's possession.

4. University Committee on Housing, "Memorandum to President Olpin and the Board of Regents," December 2, 1945, Olpin Presidential Records, box 10, University Archives.

5. Paul W. Hodson, *Crisis on Campus: The Exciting Years of Campus Development at the University of Utah* (Salt Lake City: Keeban Corporation, 1987), 275–79.

6. Joan Cartan, interview with A. Ray Olpin, November 24, 1981, Salt Lake City, Everett L. Cooley Oral History Project, tape U-1569, transcript, p. 13, Special Collections, J. Willard Marriott Library, University of Utah, Salt Lake City.

7. Carl J. Christensen to Dean William Stuart Nelson, January 21, 1958, Olpin Presidential Records, box 116, University Archives.

8. University of Utah Board of Regents, minutes of meeting on June 14, 1948, Board of Regents Records, University Archives.

9. Cartan interview, 14.

10. Ibid.

11. Ibid.

12. Ibid.

13. Charles G. Hibbard, "Fort Douglas, 1862–1916: Pivotal Link on the Western Frontier" (PhD diss., University of Utah, 1980).

14. Herbert B. Maw, telegram to General Dwight D. Eisenhower, June 28, 1946, Olpin Presidential Records, box 2, University Archives.

15. G. Homer Durham, "The Close of the First Century: Prologue to the University to Come," September 20, 1958, pp. 5, Olpin Presidential Records, box 125, University Archives. This brief history of Olpin's administration through 1958 was written as a substitute postscript to Ralph V. Chamberlain's *The University of Utah: A History of Its First Hundred Years, 1850 to 1950,* published by the University of Utah Press in 1960. It was not included in the published volume.

16. Hodson, *Crisis on Campus,* 27.

17. Ibid.

18. Minutes of the Dean's Council meeting, February 20, 1946, University Archives.

19. Seibert W. Mote to A. Ray Olpin, September 22, 1945, Olpin Presidential Records, box 2, University Archives.

20. "Olpin Sees Research as Industry Basis," *Salt Lake Telegram,* March 14, 1946.

21. A. Ray Olpin, president's postwar report, n.d. (circa 1951), pp. 1–6, Olpin Presidential Records, box 78, University Archives.

22. A. Ray Olpin to Senator Arthur V. Watkins, May 22, 1947, Olpin Presidential Records, box 29, University Archives.

23. Partridge interview.

24. University of Utah Board of Regents, minutes of meeting on June 19, 1947, Board of Regents Records, University Archives.

25. Partridge interview.

26. Cyril M. Whitlow to A. Ray Olpin, January 6, 1947, Olpin Presidential Records, box 29, University Archives.

27. John B. Matheson Jr. to Dean John L. Ballif, May 15, 1947, Olpin Presidential Records, box 40, University Archives.

28. "Olpin Expresses Concern over Vet Project Ban," *Salt Lake Tribune,* Dec. 24, 1946, 13.

29. John L. Ballif to A. Ray Olpin, July 17, 1947, Olpin Presidential Records, box 40, University Archives.

30. LaVelle Eastman, interview by the author, May 2, 2006, Salt Lake City.

31. Partridge interview.

CHAPTER 2

BRINGING PROFESSORS ALONG

1. Henry P. Plenk, *Medicine in the Beehive State, 1940–1990* (Salt Lake City: Utah Medical Association, 1992), 3–59.

2. A. Ray Olpin to Carroll L. Shartle, August 13, 1948, Olpin Presidential Records, box 52, University Archives, University of Utah, Salt Lake City (hereafter cited as University Archives).

3. G. Homer Durham, "The Close of the First Century: Prologue to the University to Come," September 20, 1958, pp. 1–13, Olpin Presidential Records, box 125, University Archives.

4. A. Ray Olpin to Henry Eyring, January 7, 1946, Olpin Presidential Records, box 6, University Archives.

5. University of Utah Board of Regents, minutes of meeting on April 12, 1946, Board of Regents Records, University Archives.

6. A. Ray Olpin to Carl Christensen, June 22, 1946, Olpin Presidential Records, box 9, University Archives.

7. University of Utah Board of Regents, minutes of meeting on June 22, 1946, Board of Regents Records, University Archives.

8. Everett L. Cooley, interview with Paul Hodson, June 16, 1986, Everett L. Cooley Oral History Project, interview #155, Special Collections, J. Willard Marriott Library, University of Utah, Salt Lake City (hereafter cited as Special Collections).

9. A. Ray Olpin to Henry Eyring, May 13, 1946, Henry Eyring Faculty File, accession 526, folder 1, University Archives.

10. H. S. Taylor, address at Princeton University in honor of Henry Eyring, August 2, 1946, Henry Eyring Papers, box 23, University Archives.

11. Henry Eyring to A. Ray Olpin, March 29, 1946, Henry Eyring Faculty File, accession 526, folder 1, University Archives..

12. Edward M. Eyring, "University of Utah; the Chemistry Department; 1946-2000," Special Collections.

13. Elinore Partridge, interview with A. Ray Olpin, January 9, 1975, Salt Lake City, notes in author's possession.

14. John E. Christensen, "Impact of World War II," in *Utah's History,* ed. Richard D. Poll, Thomas G. Alexander, Eugene E. Campbell, and David E. Miller (Logan: Utah State University Press, 1989), 511–14.

15. Carl J. Christensen to Dean William Stuart Nelson, January 21, 1958, Olpin Presidential Records, box 116, University Archives.

16. A. Ray Olpin, "1947—a Year of Opportunity for Utah," speech to the Utah State Bar, January 4, 1947, Olpin Presidential Records, box 20, University Archives.

17. Avard Fairbanks to A. Ray Olpin, October 31, 1946, Olpin Presidential Records, box 23, University Archives.

18. Avard Fairbanks to A. Ray Olpin, July 22, 1950, Olpin Presidential Records, box 74, University Archives.

19. Harold W. Bentley to A. Ray Olpin, September 14, 1947, Olpin Presidential Records, box 32, University Archives.

20. A. Ray Olpin to Harold W. Bentley, February 12, 1948, Olpin Presidential Records, box 47, University Archives.

21. Bentley to Olpin.

22. Olpin to Bentley.

23. University of Utah Board of Regents, minutes of meeting on February 15, 1946, Board of Regents Records, University Archives.

24. Partridge interview. Olpin retold this story several times in interviews. It was repeated to me also by William Mulder in an interview I did on February 1, 2006.

25. A. Ray Olpin, speech at the seventy-ninth commencement of the University of Utah, June 12, 1948, Olpin Presidential Records, box 50, University Archives.

26. Christensen to Nelson.

27. Paul W. Hodson, interview by the author, February 7, 2006, South Jordan.

28. W. Conrad Fernelius to A. Ray Olpin, May 24, 1946, Olpin Presidential Records, box 9, University Archives.

29. Samuel S. Kistler, "Report to the President on the Building Needs of the College of Engineering," August 15, 1954, Olpin Presidential Records, box 96, University Archives.

30. Dietrich K. Gehmlich, *A History of the College of Engineering: Historical Notes Relating to the Teaching of Engineering at the University of Utah, 1850 to 2000* (Salt Lake City: University of Utah, 2003), available online at http://www.coe.utah.edu/includes/documents/history.pdf

31. Parry D. Sorensen, former University of Utah public-relations director, interview by the author, April 27, 2006, Salt Lake City.

32. Ibid.

33. Fernelius to Olpin.

34. A. Ray Olpin to W. Conrad Fernelius, May 29, 1946, Olpin Presidential Records, box 9, University Archives.

35. A. Ray Olpin, speech at the University of Utah centenary, February 27, 1950, Olpin Presidential Records, box 58, University Archives.

36. A. Ray Olpin, Founder's Day speech, February 10, 1947, Olpin Presidential Records, box 36, University Archives.

37. Hays Gorey, "Olpin of University of Utah Retires," September 13, 1963, "Dispatches from *Time* Magazine Correspondents," second series, 1956–68, Harvard University Library, Cambridge, Massachusetts.

38. American Association of University Professors, *Report of the Committee of Inquiry on Conditions at the University of Utah,* July 1915, pp. 1–82, Special Collections. Whether Utah was established before any other western university is actually disputed.

<h2 style="text-align:center">CHAPTER 3
BATTLING THE WILL OF GOVERNOR LEE</h2>

1. "Solon Raps Lee Attacks as Veto Preparation," *Deseret News,* February 28, 1949.

2. "School Chiefs Contend State Shirking Duty," *Ogden Standard Examiner,* January 28, 1949.

3. Ray E. Spendlove to J. Bracken Lee, March 4, 1949, Olpin Presidential Records, box 56, University Archives, University of Utah, Salt Lake City (hereafter cited as University Archives).

4. *The State University in American Education, Centennial Commemoration Proceedings* (Salt Lake City: University of Utah Press, 1950), 63, Special Collections, J. Willard Marriott Library, University of Utah, Salt Lake City (hereafter cited as Special Collections).

5. Ibid., 61.

6. A. Ray Olpin, "My Daily Journal," July 16, 1951, Olpin Presidential Records, accession 219, box 2, University Archives.

7. Frank Browning to J. Bracken Lee, March 10, 1951, Olpin Presidential Records, box 84, University Archives.

8. A. Ray Olpin, "My Daily Journal," March 10, 1951, Olpin Presidential Records, accession 219, box 2, University Archives.

9. Parry D. Sorensen, former University of Utah public-relations director, interview by the author, April 27, 2006, Salt Lake City.

10. Olpin, "My Daily Journal," July 16, 1951.

11. A. Ray Olpin, speech to the Salt Lake Advertising Club, October 22, 1947, Olpin Presidential Records, box 36, University Archives.

12. J. Bracken Lee to A. Ray Olpin, April 26, 1951, Olpin Presidential Records, box 81, University Archives.

13. J. Bracken Lee to Sterling W. Sill, June 19, 1951, Olpin Presidential Records, box 81, University Archives.

14. A. Ray Olpin to J. Bracken Lee, May 16, 1951: Olpin Presidential Records, box 81, University Archives.

15. Benjamin Fine, "Colleges Disclose Enrollment Loss," *New York Times,* November 25, 1950.

16. Sterling W. Sill to J. Bracken Lee, June 27, 1951, Olpin Presidential Records, box 81, University Archives.

17. Olpin to Lee, May 16, 1951.

18. A. Ray Olpin, "My Daily Journal, March 6, 1951, Olpin Presidential Records, box 1, University Archives.

19. Ibid.

20. J. Bracken Lee to A. Ray Olpin, March 7, 1951, Olpin Presidential Records, box 81, University Archives.

21. A. Ray Olpin to J. Bracken Lee, March 12, 1951, Olpin Presidential Records, box 81, University Archives.

22. Dennis L. Lythgoe, *Let 'em Holler: A Political Biography of J. Bracken Lee* (Salt Lake City: Utah State Historical Society, 1982), 101.

23. J. Bracken Lee, "Message of Governor J. Bracken Lee to the First Special Session of the Twenty-Ninth Legislature of the State of Utah," June 4, 1951, p. 3, Olpin Presidential Records, box 81, University Archives.

24. *Laws of the State of Utah* (First special session of the twenty-ninth legislature, June 4–16, 1951).

25. Lee to Sill, June 19, 1951.

26. Sill to Lee, June 27, 1951.

27. Harold W. Simpson, press release from the office of Governor J. Bracken Lee, June 23, 1951, Olpin Presidential Records, box 82, University Archives.

28. Everett L. Cooley, interview with Paul Hodson, June 16, 1986, Everett L. Cooley Oral History Project, Special Collections.

29. Paul W. Hodson, "Memorandum on Systematization of Work in the President's Office," September 19, 1950, Olpin Presidential Records, box 78, University Archives.

30. Paul W. Hodson, *Crisis on Campus: The Exciting Years of Campus Development at the University of Utah* (Salt Lake City: Keeban Corporation, 1987), 9.

31. University of Utah Board of Regents, minutes of meeting on July 2, 1951, Board of Regents Records, University Archives.

32. A. Ray Olpin, "My Daily Journal," July 2, 1951, Olpin Presidential Records, accession 219, box 2, University Archives.

33. Stewart M. Lowry to William J. O'Connor, December 26, 1951, Olpin Presidential Records, box 82, University Archives.

34. Ibid.

35. Paul W. Hodson, "Memorandum to President A. Ray Olpin," March 28, 1952, pp. 1–3, Olpin Presidential Records, box 82, University Archives.

36. Booz, Allen, and Hamilton, *Survey of Administration,* July 15, 1952, Olpin Presidential Records, box 82, University Archives.

37. Richard A. Squires, "Lee, O'Connor Commend Survey of U.," *Salt Lake Tribune,* August 12, 1952, 11.

38. Handwritten notes on A. Ray Olpin's notepaper inserted in bound *Survey of Administration,* in author's possession.

39. University of Utah Board of Regents, "Statement in Response to the Booz, Allen, and Hamilton Administrative Survey of the University of Utah," August 1952, Board of Regents Records, box 89, University Archives.

40. A. Ray Olpin, "My Daily Journal," August 5, 1952, Olpin Presidential Records, box 3, University Archives.

41. A. Ray Olpin, "Memo in Response to the Booz, Allen, and Hamilton Report," August 5, 1952, Olpin Presidential Records, box 82, University Archives.

42. John S. Wood to A. Ray Olpin, June 9, 1949, Olpin Presidential Records, box 44, University Archives.

43. Ibid.

44. Richard B. Kennan to A. Ray Olpin, June 17, 1949, Olpin Presidential Records, box 44, University Archives.

45. Faculty Council Committee on Academic Freedom and Tenure, minutes of the meeting on August 17, 1949, University Archives.

46. James E. P. Toman to A. Ray Olpin, June 29, 1949, Olpin Presidential Records, box 63, University Archives.

47. James E. P. Toman to Faculty Council Committee on Academic Freedom and Tenure, June 30, 1949, Olpin Presidential Records, box 63, University Archives.

48. *Utah Code Annotated,* law 75-1-14 (1943).

49. Horace W. Davenport to A. Ray Olpin, July 5, 1949, Olpin Presidential Records, box 63, University Archives.

50. Dr. Louis S. Goodman to A. Ray Olpin, July 7, 1949, Olpin Presidential Records, box 63, University Archives.

51. University of Utah Board of Regents, minutes of the executive session on July 7, 1949, Board of Regenrs Records, University Archives.

52. Faculty Council Committee on Academic Freedom and Tenure, "Report of the Faculty Council Committee on Academic Freedom and Tenure as Approved by the Faculty Council," October 6, 1949, Olpin Presidential Records, box 48, University Archives.

53. O. Meredith Wilson to members of the Faculty Council Committee on Academic Freedom and Tenure, August 16, 1949, Olpin Presidential Records, box 48, University Archives.

54. University of Utah Board of Regents, minutes of the Executive Committee meeting on September 8, 1949, Board of Regents Records, University Archives.

55. University of Utah Board of Regents, minutes of the special session of the Executive Committee, October 17, 1949, Board of Regents Records, University Archives.

56. Ibid.

57. Ibid.

58. Rulon S. Howells to A. Ray Olpin, September 19, 1949, Olpin Presidential Records, box 57, University Archives.

59. Paul W. Hodson, cablegram to A. Ray Olpin, November 11, 1949, Olpin Presidential Records, box 63, University Archives.

60. Hector C. Sabelli, ed., *Chemical Modulation of Brain Function—A Tribute to J. E. P. Toman* (New York: Raven Press Publishers, 1973), 9–14.

CHAPTER 4
SETTING SIGHTS ON WASHINGTON

1. A. Ray Olpin to Howard L. Bevis, July 27, 1945, Olpin Presidential Records, box 2, University Archives, University of Utah, Salt Lake City (hereafter cited as University Archives).

2. "Research Projects Secret," *Ohio State University Monthly,* January 1942, copy in author's possession.

3. "Research Imperative," *Ohio State University Monthly,* February 1942, copy in author's possession.

4. Howard L. Bevis to the Special Committee for the Selection of the President, July 30, 1945, Board of Regents Records, box 12 University Archives.

5. "Research Imperative."

6. Olpin to Bevis.

7. Elinore Partridge, interview with A. Ray Olpin, January 9, 1975, Salt Lake City, notes in author's possession. Olpin told Partridge, "I like this definition because it indicates that research is an attitude of mind, a thinking process.… It makes research an upward reach.… it places a premium on the practical without discounting the theoretical."

8. Faculty Committee to Assist the Board of Regents in the Selection of the President, report presented to the Board of Regents, August 3, 1945, Olpin Presidential Records, box 5, University Archives.

9. A. Ray Olpin to LeRoy Cowles, May 31, 1945, Olpin Presidential Records, box 6, University Archives.

10. Ralph V. Chamberlin, *The University of Utah: A History of Its First Hundred Years, 1850 to 1950* (Salt Lake City: University of Utah Press, 1960) 476–77.

11. W. Leary, O. Tugman, E. Erickson, R. Lewis, and S. Angleman to A. Ray Olpin, July 28, 1945, Olpin Presidential Records, box 12, University Archives.

12. A. Ray Olpin to the Special Committee for the Selection of the President, July 30, 1945, Board of Regents Records, box 12, University Archives.

13. Bevis to the Special Committee

14. Ohio State University, file on Albert Ray Olpin, biographical files, 1945, Ohio State University Archives, Columbus, Ohio, copy in Olpin Presidential Records, accession 24, box 2, University Archives.

15. Louis Raths to the Faculty Committee to Assist the Board of Regents in the Selection of a President, July 31, 1945, Board of Regents Records, box 12, University Archives.

16. Harry E. Nold to the Special Committee for the Selection of the President, July 30, 1945, Board of Regents Records, box 12, University Archives.

17. Harlan Hatcher to the Special Committee for the Selection of the President, July 31, 1945, Board of Regents Records, box 12, University Archives.

18. Raths to the Faculty Committee

19. Ibid.

20. University of Utah Board of Regents, minutes of meeting on July 27, 1945, Board of Regents Records, University Archives.

21. Arthur Gaeth, "Choosing the New President of the University of Utah," broadcast on the Intermountain Radio Network, August 2, 1945, transcript in Board of Regents Records, box 12, University Archives.

22. Ohio State University, Olpin file.

23. University of Utah Board of Regents, minutes of meeting on August 10, 1945, Board of Regents Records, University Archives.

24. University of Utah Board of Regents, minutes of meeting on September 3, 1945, Board of Regents Records, University Archives.

25. "Olpin Asserts Research Is Key to Work," *Salt Lake Telegram,* February 6, 1946.

26. A. Ray Olpin, "Acknowledgement," a speech given at his inauguration, October 16, 1946, p. 57, Olpin Presidential Records, box 6, University Archives.

27. Ibid.

28. A. Ray Olpin to Clyde Williams, November 28, 1950, Olpin Presidential Records, box 75, University Archives.

29. A. Ray Olpin, *Report of the President, 1950–51,* Special Collections, J. Willard Marriott Library, University of Utah, Salt Lake City (hereafter cited as Special Collections).

30. Elmo Morgan, "Procedures for Cooperative Research Contracts," November 2, 1951, Olpin Presidential Records, box 86, University Archives.

31. A. Ray Olpin, *Report of the President, 1953–54,* Special Collections.

32. Assistant Secretary for Environment, Safety, and Health, *Human Radiation Experiments Associated with the U.S. Department of Energy and Its Predecessors* (Washington, DC: U.S. Department of Energy, 1995), 186–87.

33. Assistant Secretary for Environment, Safety, and Health, *Human Radiation Experiments: The DOE Roadmap to the Story and the Records* (Washington, DC: U.S. Department of Energy, 1995), 287–88.

34. Elmo R. Morgan to Dr. John C. Bugher, May 23, 1955, Elmo Morgan Papers, accession 25, box 2, University Archives.

35. Elmo R. Morgan to A. Ray Olpin, December 30, 1953, Olpin Presidential Records, box 95, University Archives.

36. Olpin, *Report of the President, 1953–54.*

37. Elmo R. Morgan to A. Ray Olpin, August 17, 1955, Olpin Presidential Records, box 110, University Archives.

38. Paul W. Hodson, *Crisis on Campus: The Exciting Years of Campus Development at the University of Utah* (Salt Lake City: Keeban Corporation, 1987), ii.

39. J. W. Athens, A. M. Mauer, H. Ashenbrucker, G. E. Cartwright, and M. M. Wintrobe, "A Method for Labeling Leukocytes with Diisopropylfluorosphosphate (DFP-32)," *Blood: The Journal of Hematology* 14, no.4 (April 1959): 303–33.

40. Carl J. Christensen, "Preliminary Report to the President from Cooperative Research, July 1, 1961–June 30, 1962," Olpin Presidential Records, box 142, University Archives.

41. Melvin A. Cook, "Report on Institute of Metals and Explosives Research," October 1963, Melvin A. Cook Faculty File, University Archives.

42. Dietrich K. Gehmlich, *A History of the College of Engineering: Historical Notes Relating to the Teaching of Engineering at the University of Utah, 1850 to 2000* (Salt Lake City: University of Utah, 2003), available online at http://www.coe.utah.edu/includes/documents/history.pdf

43. A. Ray Olpin to Melvin A. Cook, July 10, 1963, Olpin Presidential Records, box 148, University Archives.

44. Milton E. Wadsworth to Daniel J. Dykstra, January 15, 1962, Melvin A. Cook Faculty File, University Archives.

45. A. Ray Olpin, *Report of the President, 1959–60,* Special Collections.

46. Bruce H. Jensen, "University of Utah: A History of Campus Development," 1973, MS 445, Special Collections.

47. A. Ray Olpin to H. N. Eskildson, February 8, 1962, Olpin Presidential Records, box 144, University Archives.

48. Ewart A. Swinyard, "University Research Committee Activities, 1960–61," Olpin Presidential Records, box 136, University Archives.

Chapter 5
Spreading Worldly Ambition

1. A. Ray Olpin, "Youth Peace Corps Proposal," paper presented at the sixth Far Western Conference of Fulbright Scholars, sponsored by the California Institute of Technology in cooperation with the Committee on International Exchange of Persons of the Conference Board of Associated Research Councils, Pasadena, March 23–26, 1961, p. 1, Olpin Presidential Records, box 137, University Archives, University of Utah, Salt Lake City (hereafter cited as University Archives).

2. Paul Cracroft, "Olpin-San: Mover of Mountains," *Utah Alumnus* 43, no. 3 (spring 1967): 11–17.

3. Boyer Jarvis to Shinichi Okajima, June 25, 1963, Olpin Presidential Records, box 148, University Archives.

4. A. Ray Olpin, untitled article, *Utah Alumnus* 36, no. 2 (1959), copy in author's possession.

5. A. Ray Olpin, "Discussion on the International Relations of American Universities," paper presented at the meeting of the National Association of State Universities, 1951, Olpin Presidential Records, box 71, University Archives.

6. Arthur L. Beeley, "Notes for President Olpin on the Institute of World Affairs," April 27, 1951, Olpin Presidential Records, box 77, University Archives.

7. Sam Rich, former Institute of International Studies director, interview by the author, August 18, 2006, Salt Lake City.

8. A. Ray Olpin, *Report of the President, 1963,* Special Collections, J. Willard Marriott Library, University of Utah, Salt Lake City (hereafter cited as Special Collections).

9. William Mulder quoted in "Center for Language and Intercultural Studies: A New Approach," *Utah Alumnus* 36, no. 1 (October 1959): 4–5.

10. William Mulder, "Area Studies at the University of Utah," November 26, 1962, Olpin Presidential Records, box 147, University Archives.

11. William Mulder, former Institute of American Studies director, interview by the author, February 1, 2006, Salt Lake City.

12. Sterling McMurrin to G. Homer Durham, April 5, 1957, Olpin Presidential Records, box 117, University Archives.

13. Mulder interview.

14. A. Ray Olpin, "Discussion on the International Relations of American Universities."

15. A. Ray Olpin, Travel Journal, August 7, 1953, Cairo, Olpin Presidential Records, accession 219, box 12, University Archives.

16. Ibid.

17. Roy V. Peel to A. Ray Olpin, March 3, 1959, Olpin Presidential Records, box 120, University Archives.

18. Everett L. Cooley, interview with Aziz S. Atiya, 1985, Everett L. Cooley Oral History Project, tape 42, Special Collections.

19. Elinore Partridge, interview with A. Ray Olpin, January 9, 1975, Salt Lake City, notes in author's possession.

20. A. Ray Olpin, "A Brief Report on Conditions in New Zealand and Japan as Observed by Albert Ray Olpin, President of the University of Utah, during a Tour Sponsored by the Leaders and Specialists Branch, Educational Exchange Division, U.S. Department of State, August–October 1953, with Recommendations for Improving Public Relations, Particularly in Japan," p. 18, Olpin Presidential Records, box 97, University Archives.

21. G. Homer Durham, "Memorandum on the Olpin Plan of International Studies," April 10, 1958, Olpin Presidential Records, box 117, University Archives.

22. Sterling McMurrin to A. Ray Olpin, December 17, 1958, Olpin Presidential Records, box 120, University Archives.

23. "Peace: By Precept and Example," *Deseret News,* June 17, 1958, A16.

24. Olpin, "A Brief Report on Conditions," 11.

25. Ibid., 15.

26. A. Ray Olpin, "International Friendships Are Made at the Grassroots Level," speech, n.d., p. 5, Box 109, Olpin Presidential Records University Archives.

27. A. Ray Olpin, "Youth Peace Corps Proposal," p. 2.

28. A. Ray Olpin, "My Daily Journal," January 28–29, 1959, Olpin Presidential Records, box 7, University Archives.

29. J. W. Fulbright to A. Ray Olpin, August 26, 1959, Olpin Presidential Records, box 130, University Archives.

30. A. Ray Olpin to Senator Wallace F. Bennett, June 24, 1958, Olpin Presidential Records, box 117, University Archives.

31. Wallace F. Bennett to A. Ray Olpin, June 30, 1958, Olpin Presidential Records, box 117, University Archives.

32. Stephen Duggan, *A Professor at Large* (New York: The Macmillan Company, 1943), 18.

33. Harold W. Bentley, "Memorandum on a Youth Service Corps Abroad, Together with a Draft of a Proposed Bill to Authorize Such a Corps, and a Recommendation by Dr. A. Ray Olpin, President of the University," 1960, part 1, p. 6, Academic Vice President, 1959–60, accession 3, Box 22, Olpin Plan of International Studies, 22-10, University Archives.

34. A. Ray Olpin, "My Daily Journal," December 9, 1960, Olpin Presidential Records, box 8, University Archives.

35. Dean's Council, minutes of the meeting on December 22, 1960, University Archives.

36. Samuel P. Hayes, "An International Peace Corps: The Promise and the Problems," draft copy 1, March 1961, p. 18, Samuel P. Hayes Collection, box 2, folder 2, #101, John F. Kennedy Presidential Library, Boston.

37. A. Ray Olpin, "My Daily Journal," March 22, 1961, Olpin Presidential Records, accession 219, box 8, University Archives.

38. "Shriver Asks U. to Assist in Peace Corps," *Deseret News,* April 14, 1961.

39. Harold W. Bentley, "Peace Corps Training Program for Tunisia and Morocco, a Final Report," 1964, Bentley Papers, accession 195, box 7, University Archives.

40. A. Ray Olpin to Senator Wallace F. Bennett, May 13, 1960, Olpin Presidential Records, box 129, University Archives.

41. Philip B. Price, Ethiopian trip journal, February 21, 1960, p. 2, Middle East Collection, J. Willard Marriott Library, University of Utah, Salt Lake City.

42. William H. Josephson, "Official Use Only," Correspondence and Memoranda, February–June 1962, William Josephson chronological file 1962, roll 9, frame 1116, John F. Kennedy Presidential Library, Boston.

43. Harold Bentley to A. Ray Olpin, May 3, 1962. Addis Ababa. Olpin Presidential Records, Box 143, University Archives.

44. A. Ray Olpin, "An Amazing Decade of Television Development," report to the Ford Foundation and Institute of International Education, 1963, Olpin Presidential Records, University Archives.

45. Harold Bentley to A. Ray Olpin, May 25, 1962, Olpin Presidential Records, box 143, University Archives.

46. A. Ray Olpin, "Cosmopolitan Provincialism Utah!" speech to the Newcomen Society in North America, October 4, 1955, reprinted by Princeton University Press, February 1956, p. 21, Olpin Presidential Records, box 100, University Archives. Olpin delivered the address, detailing the history of the University of Utah, at the 1955 Utah dinner of the society, held in the Empire Room of the Hotel Utah, where he was the guest of honor.

47. Ibid., 9.

48. Ibid., 21.

49. Ibid., 24.

Chapter 6
Quelling the Medical Crisis

1. University of Utah Board of Regents, minutes of meeting on March 8, 1946, Board of Regents Records, University Archives, University of Utah, Salt Lake City (hereafter cited as University Archives).

2. Clarence Bamberger, "First Annual Report of the Utah State Hospital for Poliomelitis and Other Crippling Children's Diseases to the Governor and Legislature," 1945, Olpin Presidential Records, box 10, University Archives.

3. Ibid.

4. University of Utah Board of Regents, minutes of meeting on December 13, 1946, Board of Regents Records, University Archives.

5. Board of Regents, minutes of March 8, 1946.

6. Ibid.

7. H. L. Marshall to A. Ray Olpin, June 15, 1946, Olpin Presidential Records, box 23, University Archives.

8. Leonard J. Jarcho, interview with Dr. Maxwell Wintrobe, 1970, Everett L. Cooley Oral History Project, tape 283, Special Collections, J. Willard Marriott Library, University of Utah, Salt Lake City (hereafter cited as Special Collections).

9. Marshall to Olpin.

10. H. L. Marshall, *Summarized History of the University of Utah College of Medicine,* June 1, 1957, pp. 1–4, Olpin Presidential Records, box 116, University Archives. The report includes organizational descriptions, cost summaries, medical and teaching caseloads from 1939 to 1959, and a summary of terminations in 1958–59, which indicates that eight doctors left the university faculty to "accept other employment at much higher salary."

11. Henry P. Plenk, *Medicine in the Beehive State, 1940–1990* (Salt Lake City: Utah Medical Association, 1992), 6.

12. A. Ray Olpin, "Cosmopolitan Provincialism Utah!" speech to the Newcomen Society in North America, October 4, 1955, p. 9, reprinted by Princeton University Press, February 1956.

13. Plenk, *Medicine in the Beehive State,* 9.

14. Jarcho interview with Wintrobe.

15. Ibid.

16. Hans Hecht to Paul W. Hodson, December 19, 1957, Olpin Presidential Records, box 115, University Archives.

17. Mary P. Chachas, ed., *The Gift of Health Goes On: A History of the University of Utah Medical Center* (Salt Lake City: Office of Community Relations, University of Utah Health Sciences Center, 1990), 17.

18. Dr. George L. Veasy, founding medical director of Primary Children's Medical Center, interview by the author, March 7, 2007, Salt Lake City.

19. Philip B. Price, "A Statement Concerning the Medical Center, January 15, 1957, p. 4, Olpin Presidential Records, box 128, University Archives.

20. Ibid, 2.

21. A. Ray Olpin, *Report of the President, 1959–60,* Special Collections.

22. Veasy interview.

23. Whitney Blair Young, "A History of the University of Utah College of Medicine" (PhD diss., University of Kansas, 1963).

24. *Medical Center News* (University of Utah) 1, no. 1 (April 1, 1962): 1.

25. Olpin, *Report of the President, 1959–60.*

26. Helen Rae Olpin Snow Callahan, interview by the author, December 12, 2006, Salt Lake City.

CHAPTER 7
ORCHESTRATING THE ARTS

1. Lowell M. Durham, "Intermission Remarks during Special Chamber Music Festival Concert Honoring President Emeritus A. Ray Olpin," February 7, 1971, copy in author's possession.

2. G. Homer Durham, "The Close of the First Century: Prologue to the University to Come," September 20, 1958, p. 10, Olpin Presidential Records, box 125, University Archives, University of Utah, Salt Lake City (hereafter cited as University Archives).

3. Everett L. Cooley, interview with Boyer Jarvis, 1983, Everett L. Cooley Oral History Project, #22, Special Collections, J. Willard Marriott Library, University of Utah, Salt Lake City (hereafter cited as Special Collections).

4. Durham, "Close of the First Century."

5. A. Ray Olpin, "My Daily Journal," April 12, 1948, Olpin Presidential Records, box 1, University Archives.

6. Winnifred Margetts, interview with Lowell M. Durham, Everett L. Cooley Oral History Project, 1987, #96, Special Collections.

7. Paul W. Hodson, *Crisis on Campus: The Exciting Years of Campus Development at the University of Utah* (Salt Lake City: Keeban Corporation, 1987).

8. Avard Fairbanks to A. Ray Olpin, April 24, 1953, Olpin Presidential Records, box 96, University Archives.

9. Margetts interview with Durham.

10. Ronald C. Allen, "A History of the Utah Museum of Fine Arts" (master's thesis, University of Utah, 2005).

11. A. Ray Olpin, "My Daily Journal," May 6, 1951, Olpin Presidential Records, box 1, University Archives.

12. A. Ray Olpin, "My Daily Journal," July 16, 1951, Olpin Presidential Records, box 2, University Archives.

13. Allen, "History of the Utah Museum."

14. University of Utah Board of Regents, minutes of the meeting on April 14, 1952, Board of Regents Records, University Archives.

15. University of Utah Board of Regents, minutes of the meeting on March 13, 1961, Board of Regents Records, University Archives.

16. A. Ray Olpin, "My Daily Journal," March 27, 1961, Olpin Presidential Records, accession 219, box 8, University Archives.

17. "Olpin Asks Probe in U. Art Squabble," *Salt Lake Tribune,* March 17, 1961.

18. Sydney W. Angleman to A. Ray Olpin, April 7, 1961, Olpin Presidential Records, box 141, University Archives.

19. Hugh C. Smith to A. Ray Olpin, September 17, 1958, Olpin Presidential Records, box 120, University Archives.

20. A. Ray Olpin to President David O. McKay, October 27, 1958, Olpin Presidential Records, box 120, University Archives.

21. A. Ray Olpin, "My Daily Journal," October 17, 1947, Olpin Presidential Records, box 1, University Archives.

22. Faculty of the Department of Health, Physical Education, and Recreation to A. Ray Olpin, October 19, 1950, Olpin Presidential Records, box 73, University Archives.

23. Olga Maynard, "The Christensen Brothers," *Dance Magazine* 47, no. 6 (June 1973), Special Collections.

24. Karlynn Hinman, "Dr. Olpin and University Make Television First," *Daily Utah Chronicle,* March 1, 1961.

25. Gail Plummer to A. Ray Olpin, November 10, 1950, Olpin Presidential Records, box 75, University Archives.

26. "A Sound Decision," editorial, *Salt Lake Tribune,* March 21, 1953.

27. A. Ray Olpin, "The Educational Challenge in Your State and Mine," paper presented at the Biennial Convention of the National Council on State Legislation, May 18, 1957, Olpin Presidential Records, University Archives.

28. A. Ray Olpin, "Why Go on the Air?" speech to the American College Public Relations Association, June 30, 1953, Olpin Presidential Records, University Archives.

29. Durham, "Close of the First Century."

30. James C. Fletcher, *Report of the President, 1964–65,* Special Collections.

31. Paul Cracroft, "Olpin-San: Mover of Mountains," *Utah Alumnus* 43, no. 3 (spring 1967): 11–17.

CHAPTER 8
RECALLING OLPIN'S LEGACY

1. Major Kirby E. Kirkman, "Fort Douglas Land Grab" (Reserve Officers Association of the United States, Salt Lake Chapter newsletter, November 20, 1959), Olpin Presidential Records, box 128, University Archives, University of Utah, Salt Lake City (hereafter cited as University Archives).

2. A. Ray Olpin, "My Daily Journal," June 8, 1964, Olpin Presidential Records, box 11, University Archives.

3. J. Bracken Lee to A. Ray Olpin, December 16, 1968, Olpin Presidential Records, accession 24, box 152, University Archives.

BIBLIOGRAPHY

Books, Articles, and Newspapers

Assistant Secretary for Environment, Safety, and Health. *Human Radiation Experiments Associated with the U.S. Department of Energy and Its Predecessors.* Washington, DC: U.S. Department of Energy, 1995.

———. *Human Radiation Experiments: The DOE Roadmap to the Story and the Records.* Washington, DC: U.S. Department of Energy, 1995.

Athens, J. W., A. M. Mauer, H. Ashenbrucker, G. E. Cartwright, and M. M. Wintrobe. "A Method for Labeling Leukocytes with Diisopropylfluorosphosphate (DFP-32)." *Blood: The Journal of Hematology* 14, no. 4 (April 1959): 303–33.

"Center for Language and Intercultural Studies: A New Approach." *Utah Alumnus* 36, no. 1 (October 1959): 4–5.

Chachas, Mary P., ed. *The Gift of Health Goes On: A History of the University of Utah Medical Center.* Salt Lake City: Office of Community Relations, University of Utah Health Sciences Center, 1960.

Chamberlain, Ralph V. *The University of Utah: A History of Its First Hundred Years, 1850 to 1950.* Salt Lake City: University of Utah Press, 1960.

Christensen, John E. "Impact of World War II." In *Utah's History,* edited by Richard D. Poll, Thomas G. Alexander, Eugene E. Campbell, and David E. Miller, 497–515. Logan: Utah State University Press, 1989.

Cracroft, Paul. 1967. "Olpin-San: Mover of Mountains." *Utah Alumnus* 43, no. 3 (spring 1967): 11–17.

Duggan, Stephen. *A Professor at Large.* New York: The Macmillan Company, 1943.

Fine, Benjamin. "Colleges Disclose Enrollment Loss." *New York Times,* November 25, 1950.

Hinman, Karlynn. "Dr. Olpin and University Make Television First." *Daily Utah Chronicle,* March 1, 1961.

Hodson, Paul W. *Crisis on Campus: The Exciting Years of Campus Development at the University of Utah.* Salt Lake City: Keeban Corporation, 1987.

Laws of the State of Utah. First special session of the twenty-ninth legislature, June 4–16, 1951.

Lythgoe, Dennis L. *Let 'em Holler: A Political Biography of J. Bracken Lee.* Salt Lake City: Utah State Historical Society, 1982.

Maynard, Olga. "The Christensen Brothers." *Dance Magazine* 47, no. 6 (June 1973). (Copy in Special Collections, J. Willard Marriott Library, University of Utah, Salt Lake City.)

Medical Center News (University of Utah) 1, no. 1 (April 1, 1962): 1.

"Olpin Asks Probe in U. Art Squabble." *Salt Lake Tribune,* March 17, 1961.

"Olpin Asserts Research Is Key to Work," *Salt Lake Telegram,* February 6, 1946.

"Olpin Expresses Concern over Vet Project Ban." *Salt Lake Tribune,* December 24, 1946, 13.

"Olpin Sees Research as Industry Basis." *Salt Lake Telegram,* March 14, 1946.

"Peace: By Precept and Example." *Deseret News.* June 17, 1958, A16.

Plenk, Henry P. *Medicine in the Beehive State, 1940–1990.* Salt Lake City: Utah Medical Association, 1992.

Sabelli, Hector C., ed. *Chemical Modulation of Brain Function—a Tribute to J. E. P. Toman.* New York: Raven Press Publishers, 1973.

"School Chiefs Contend State Shirking Duty." *Ogden Standard Examiner,* January 28, 1949.

"Shriver Asks U. to Assist in Peace Corps." *Deseret News,* April 14, 1961.

"Solon Raps Lee Attacks as Veto Preparation." *Deseret News,* February 28, 1949.

Squires, Richard A. "Lee, O'Connor Commend Survey of U." *Salt Lake Tribune,* August 12, 1952, 11.

"A Sound Decision." Editorial, *Salt Lake Tribune,* March 21, 1953.

The State University in American Education: Centennial Commemoration Proceedings, University of Utah. Salt Lake City: University of Utah Press, 1950.

Utah Code Annotated, law 75-1-14 (1943).

Unpublished Sources

Allen, Ronald C. "A History of the Utah Museum of Fine Arts." Master's thesis, University of Utah, 2005.

Callahan, Helen Rae Olpin Snow. Interview by the author, December 12, 2006.

Durham, Lowell M. "Intermission Remarks during Special Chamber Music Festival Concert Honoring President Emeritus A. Ray Olpin." February 7, 1971. Copy in author's possession.

Eastman, LaVelle. Interview by the author, May 2, 2006.

Gehmlich, Dietrich K. *A History of the College of Engineering: Historical Notes Relating to the Teaching of Engineering at the University of Utah, 1850 to 2000.* Salt Lake City: University of Utah, 2003. Available online at http://www.coe.utah.edu/includes/documents/history.pdf

Gorey, Hays. "Olpin of University of Utah Retires." September 13, 1963. "Dispatches from *Time* Magazine Correspondents." Harvard University Library, Cambridge, Massachusetts.

Hayes, Samuel P. "An International Peace Corps: The Promise and the Problems." March 1961. Samuel P. Hayes Collection, John F. Kennedy Presidential Library, Boston.

Hibbard, Charles G. "Fort Douglas, 1862–1916: Pivotal Link on the Western Frontier." PhD diss., University of Utah, 1980.

Hodson, Paul W. Interview by the author, February 7, 2006.

Josephson, William H. "Official Use Only." William Josephson Chronological File, 1962 Correspondence and Memoranda, John F. Kennedy Presidential Library, Boston.

Mulder, William. Interview by the author, February 1, 2006.

Olpin, A. Ray. "Birth and Name." "My Daily Journal." Vol. 5, 1920. Copy in author's possession

———. Handwritten notes on A. Ray Olpin's notepaper inserted in bound *Survey of Administration.* Copy in author's possession.

———. "International Friendships Are Made at the Grassroots Level." Speech, n.d. Copy in author's possession.

———. untitled article. *Utah Alumnus* 36, no. 2 (1959). Copy in author's possession.

Partridge, Elinore. Interview with A. Ray Olpin, January 9, 1975. Notes in author's possession.

Price, Philip B. Ethiopian trip journal. 1960. Middle East Collection, J. Willard Marriott Library, University of Utah, Salt Lake City.

"Research Imperative." *Ohio State University Monthly,* February 1942. Copy in author's possession.

"Research Projects Secret." *Ohio State University Monthly,* January 1942. Copy in author's possession.

Rich, Sam. Interview by the author, August 18, 2006.

Sorensen, Parry D. Interview by the author, April 27, 2006.

Veasy, Dr. George L. Interview by the author, March 7, 2007.

Young, Whitney Blair. "A History of the University of Utah College of Medicine." PhD diss., University of Kansas, 1963.

Special Collections, J. Willard Marriott Library
University of Utah, Salt Lake City.

American Association of University Professors. "Report of the Committee of Inquiry on Conditions at the University of Utah." July 1915.

Everett L. Cooley Oral History Project, including the following interviews:

Cartan, Joan. Interview with A. Ray Olpin, November 24, 1981.

Cooley, Everett L. Interview with Aziz S. Atiya, 1985.

———. Interview with Paul W. Hodson, June 16, 1986.

———. Interview with Boyer Jarvis, 1983.

Jarcho, Leonard J. Interview with Maxwell Wintrobe, 1970.

Margetts, Winnifred. Interview with Lowell Durham, 1987.

Eyring, Edward M. "University of Utah; the Chemistry Department; 1946-2000."

Fletcher, James C. *Report of the President, 1964–65.*

Jensen, Bruce H. "University of Utah: A History of Campus Development." 1973.

Olpin, A. Ray. *Report of the President, 1950–51.*

———. *Report of the President, 1953–54.*

———. *Report of the President, 1959–60.*

———. *Report of the President, 1963.*

University Archives, University of Utah, Salt Lake City

Bentley, Harold W. "Memorandum on a Youth Service Corps Abroad, Together with a Draft of a Proposed Bill to Authorize Such a Corps, and a Recommendation by Dr. A. Ray Olpin, President of the University." 1960. Bentley Papers.

———. "Peace Corps Training Program for Tunisia and Morocco, a Final Report." 1964. Bentley Papers.

Bevis, Howard L., to the Special Committee for the Selection of the President, July 30, 1945, Board of Regents Records.

Cook, Melvin A. "Report on Institute of Metals and Explosives Research," October 1963, Melvin A. Cook Faculty File.

Dean's Council. Minutes of the meetings on February 20, 1946 and December 22, 1960.

Eyring, Henry, to A. Ray Olpin, March 29, 1946, Henry Eyring Faculty File.

Faculty Council Committee on Academic Freedom and Tenure. Minutes of the meeting on August 17, 1949.

Gaeth, Arthur. "Choosing the New President of the University of Utah." Transcript of Intermountain Radio Network broadcast, August 2, 1945, Board of Regents Records.

Hatcher, Harlan, to the Special Committee for the Selection of the President, July 31, 1945, Board of Regents Records.

Morgan, Elmo R., to Dr. John C. Bugher, May 23, 1955, Elmo Morgan Papers.

Nold, Harry E., to the Special Committee for the Selection of the President, July 30, 1945, Board of Regents Records.

Olpin, A. Ray. Letter to Henry Eyring, May 13, 1946, Henry Eyring Faculty File.

———. Letter to the Special Committee for the Selection of the President, July 30, 1945, Board of Regents Records.

Raths, Louis, to the Faculty Committee to Assist the Board of Regents in the Selection of a President, July 31, 1945, Board of Regents Records.

Taylor, H. S. Address at Princeton University in honor of Henry Eyring, August 2, 1946. Henry Eyring Papers.

University of Utah Board of Regents. Minutes of various meetings from July 1945 to March 1961. Board of
    Regents Records.
———. "Statement in Response to the Booz, Allen, and Hamilton Administrative Survey of the University
    of Utah." August 1952. Board of Regents Records.
Widtsoe, John A., to Senators Reed Smoot and W. H. King, February 18, 1919.

<h3 style="text-align:center">Olpin Presidential Records</h3>

Bamberger, Clarence. "First Annual Report of the Utah State Hospital for Poliomelitis and Other
    Crippling Children's Diseases to the Governor and Legislature." 1945.
Beeley, Arthur L. "Notes for President Olpin on the Institute of World Affairs." April 27, 1951.
Booz, Allen, and Hamilton. *Survey of Administration.* July 15, 1952.
Browning, Frank, to Governor J. Bracken Lee, March 10, 1951.
Christensen, Carl J., to Dean William Stuart Nelson, January 21, 1958.
———. "Preliminary Report to the President from Cooperative Research, July 1, 1961–June 30, 1962."
Durham, G. Homer. "The Close of the First Century: Prologue to the University to Come." September 20,
    1958.
———. "Memorandum on the Olpin Plan of International Studies." April 10, 1958.
Faculty Committee to Assist the Board of Regents in the Selection of a President. Report presented to the
    Board of Regents. August 3, 1945.
Faculty Council Committee on Academic Freedom and Tenure. "Report of the Faculty Council
    Committee on Academic Freedom and Tenure as Approved by the Faculty Council." October 6,
    1949.
Hecht, Hans, to Paul W. Hodson, December 19, 1957.
Hodson, Paul W. "Memorandum on Systematization of Work in the President's Office." September 19,
    1950.
———. "Memorandum to President A. Ray Olpin." March 28, 1952.
Jarvis, Boyer, to Shinichi Okajima, June 25, 1963.
Kirkham, Major Kirby E. "Fort Douglas Land Grab." Reserve Officers Association of the United States,
    Salt Lake Chapter newsletter, November 20, 1959.
Kistler, Samuel S. "Report to the President on the Building Needs of the College of Engineering." August
    15, 1954.
Lee, J. Bracken. "Message of Governor J. Bracken Lee to the First Special Session of the Twenty-Ninth
    Legislature of the State of Utah." June 4, 1951.
———. Letter to Sterling W. Sill, June 19, 1951.
Lowry, Stewart M., to William J. O'Connor, December 26, 1951.
Marshall, H. L. *Summarized History of the University of Utah College of Medicine.* June 1, 1957.
Matheson, John B. Jr., to Dean John L. Ballif, May 15, 1947.
Maw, Herbert B. Telegram to General Dwight D. Eisenhower, June 28, 1946.
McMurrin, Sterling, to G. Homer Durham, April 5, 1957.
Morgan, Elmo R. "Procedures for Cooperative Research Contracts," November 2, 1951.
Mulder, William. "Area Studies at the University of Utah." November 26, 1962.
Ohio State University. File on Albert Ray Olpin. Biographical files, Ohio State University Archives,
    Columbus, Ohio. Copy in Olpin Presidential Records.
Olpin, A. Ray
Correspondence. Various dates, May 1945–July 1963.
"My Daily Journal." Entries from October 1947 to June 1964.
Travel Journal, August 1953.

"A Brief Report on Conditions in New Zealand and Japan as Observed by Albert Ray Olpin, President of the University of Utah, during a Tour Sponsored by the Leaders and Specialists Branch, Educational Exchange Division, U.S. Department of State, August–October 1953, with Recommendations for Improving Public Relations, Particularly in Japan."

"Acknowledgement." Speech given at his inauguration, October 16, 1946.

"An Amazing Decade of Television Development." Report to the Ford Foundation and Institute of International Education, 1963.

"Cosmopolitan Provincialism Utah!" Speech to the Newcomen Society in North America, October 4, 1955. Reprinted by Princeton University Press, 1956.

"Discussion on the International Relations of American Universities." Paper presented at the meeting of the National Association of State Universities, 1951

"The Educational Challenge in Your State and Mine." Paper presented at the Biennial Convention of the National Council on State Legislation, May 18, 1957.

Founder's Day speech, February 10, 1947.

"Memo in Response to the Booz, Allen, and Hamilton Report." August 5, 1952.

"1947—a Year of Opportunity for Utah." Speech to the Utah State Bar, January 4, 1947.

President's postwar report, n.d. (circa 1951).

Speech to the Salt Lake Advertising Club, October 22, 1947.

Speech at the seventy-ninth commencement of the University of Utah, June 12, 1948.

Speech at the University of Utah centenary, February 27, 1950.

"Why Go on the Air?" Speech to the American College Public Relations Association, June 30, 1953.

"Youth Peace Corps Proposal." Paper presented at the sixth Far Western Conference of Fulbright Scholars, sponsored by the California Institute of Technology in cooperation with the Committee on International Exchange of Persons of the Conference Board of Associated Research Councils, Pasadena, March 23–26, 1961.

 Price, Philip B. "A Statement Concerning the Medical Center." January 15, 1957.

Sill, Sterling W., to J. Bracken Lee, June 27, 1951.

Simpson, Harold W. 1951. Press release from the office of Governor J. Bracken Lee, June 23, 1951.

Spendlove, Dr. Ray E., to J. Bracken Lee, March 4, 1949.

Swinyard, Ewart A. "University Research Committee Activities, 1960–61."

Toman, James E. P., to Faculty Council Committee on Academic Freedom and Tenure, June 30, 1949.

University Committee on Housing. "Memorandum to President Olpin and the Board of Regents." December 2, 1945.

Wadsworth, Milton E., to Daniel J. Dykstra, January 15, 1962.

Wilson, O. Meredith, to members of the Faculty Council Committee on Academic Freedom and Tenure, August 16, 1949.

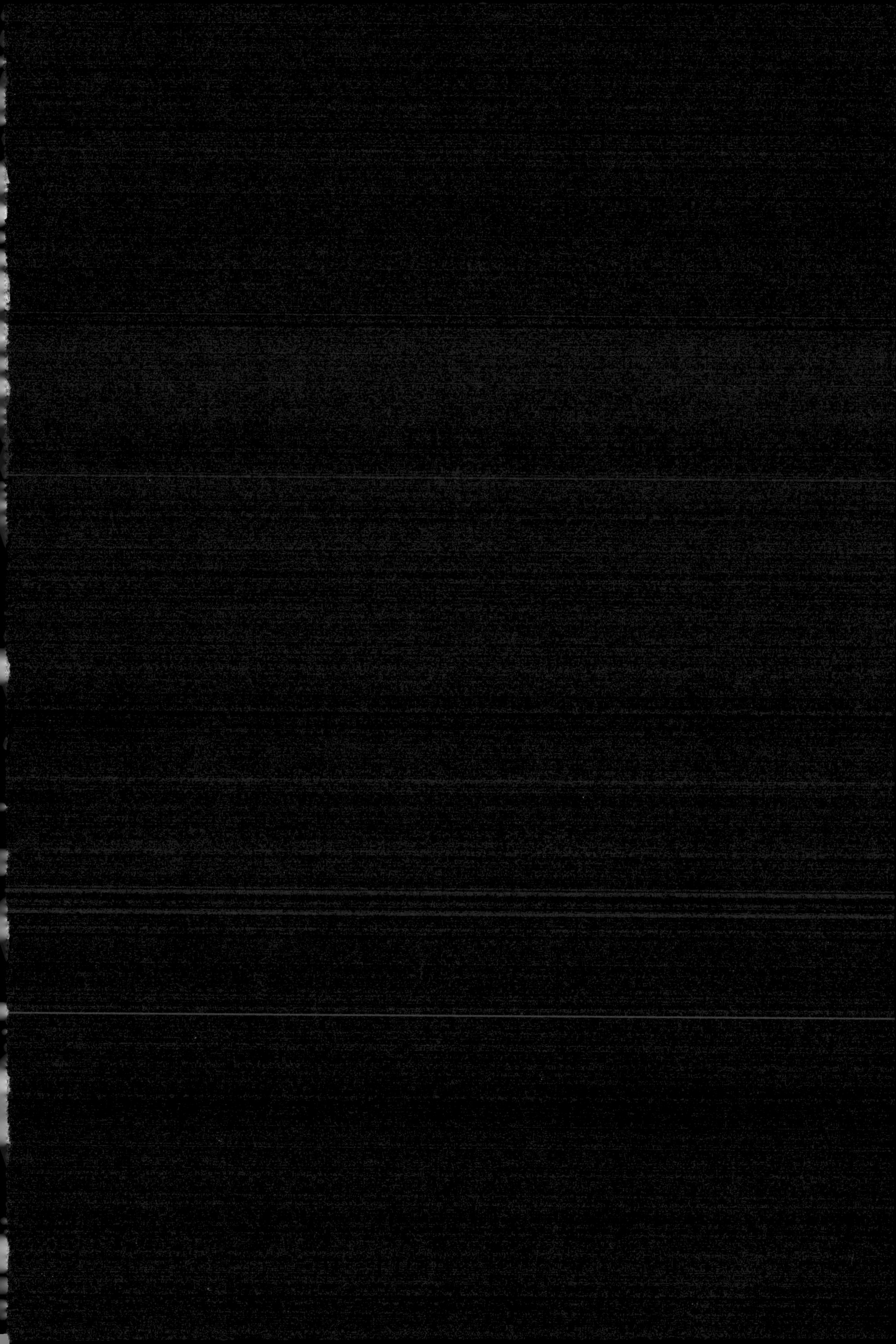